SCOTT ALLAN

REJECTION FREE FOR LIFE SERIES: BOOK 3

REJECTION REHAB

A ROADMAP TO SELF-COMPASSION, BUILDING EMOTIONAL RESILIENCE, AND CULTIVATING INNER STRENGTH

Books by Scott Allan

Empower Your Thoughts

Drive Your Destiny

Relaunch Your Life

Do the Hard Things First

Undefeated

No Punches Pulled

Fail Big

Rejection Free

Built for Stealth

www.scottallanbooks.com

Rejection Rehab

A Roadmap to Self-Compassion,
Building Emotional Resilience, and
Cultivating Inner Strength

Scott Allan

www.scottallanbooks.com

CONTENTS

Introduction: Your Journey to Rejection Resilience

Why I Wrote This Book

Like you, I've faced my share of rejections. Each "no" led me down a path of questioning my worth, my choices, and my direction in life.

But through my own journey and extensive research into rejection's impact on human psychology and behavior, I discovered something transformative: rejection, when understood and processed correctly, can become one of our most powerful catalysts for growth.

This book emerged from my deep desire to share what I've learned about transforming rejection from a source of pain into a tool for personal empowerment.

The strategies and insights within these pages aren't just theory—they're battle-tested approaches that have helped countless individuals reclaim their confidence and pursue their dreams despite the fear of rejection.

Who This Book Is For

This book is for anyone who has ever felt the sting of rejection and wondered if there might be a better way to handle it. Perhaps you're:

- A professional facing career setbacks or workplace challenges

- An artist or creator dealing with criticism and rejection of your work

- Someone navigating the complex world of relationships and social connections

- An entrepreneur or leader putting yourself out there regularly

- Anyone who wants to build stronger resilience in the face of life's "nos"

You might be dealing with fresh rejection right now, carrying the weight of past rejections, or seeking ways to handle future rejections more effectively.

Wherever you are in your journey with rejection, this book offers practical tools and insights to help you move forward with greater confidence and resilience.

How This Book Is Structured

This book is organized into four main parts, each building upon the previous one to create a comprehensive approach to handling rejection:

Part 1: Understanding Rejection: We begin by exploring the nature of rejection, its impact on our brain and body, and why it affects us so deeply.

This foundation of understanding helps normalize your experiences and prepare you for transformation.

Part 2: Transforming Rejection: Here we dive into practical strategies for processing rejection effectively, breaking free from social conditioning, and building genuine acceptance. You'll learn specific techniques for turning rejection into a tool for growth.

Part 3: Empowering Change: This section focuses on rewriting your rejection narrative, building unshakeable self-worth, and creating powerful support systems. You'll discover how to maintain forward momentum even in the face of repeated rejection.

Part 4: Building Resilience: The final section provides advanced strategies for developing lasting rejection resilience, including assertiveness skills, recovery techniques, and methods for maintaining your progress over time.

How to Read This Book

While you might be tempted to rush through these pages looking for quick solutions, I encourage you to approach this book as a journey of transformation. Here's how to get the most from your reading:

Keep a Rejection Resilience Journal: Throughout the book, you'll find prompts for reflection and exercises for practice. Dedicate a journal specifically for this work.

Writing about your experiences helps deepen your understanding and track your progress.

Practice the Exercises: Each chapter includes practical exercises designed to help you implement what you're learning.

Don't skip these—they're where real transformation happens. Think of them as building blocks for your rejection resilience.

Take Your Time: You don't need to race through this book. Each chapter builds on the previous ones, so give yourself time to process and practice.

Some learners find it helpful to spend a week with each chapter, really exploring and implementing the concepts before moving forward.

Personalize Your Approach: While the book presents a structured approach to handling rejection, feel free to adapt the techniques to your specific situation.

Pay attention to what resonates most strongly with you and focus your practice there.

Making This Journey Your Own

As you begin this book, remember that building rejection resilience is a personal journey. There's no one-size-fits-all approach to handling rejection, and your path to resilience will be as unique as you are. Use this book as a guide, taking what serves you and adapting it to fit your needs.

I encourage you to read with both an open mind and a critical eye. Question, explore, and most importantly, practice. The insights in these pages become powerful only when you put them into action in your own life.

Let's begin this journey together, transforming your relationship with rejection into something that empowers rather than diminishes you.

Turn the page when you're ready to take your first step toward greater rejection resilience.

Scott Allan

- www.scottallanbooks.com
- Join Scott Allan's Newsletter

Chapter 1: The Nature of Rejection

Think back to the last time you faced rejection. Perhaps it was a job application that went nowhere, a creative project that wasn't selected, or a relationship that ended unexpectedly.

Notice how just remembering it brings up those feelings again—the tightness in your chest, the heat in your face, the way your confidence seemed to shrink in an instant.

These visceral responses remind us that rejection isn't just a mental experience—it affects our entire being.

Take a moment now to write about your most recent rejection experience. Don't just describe what happened—capture how it felt in your body, what thoughts raced through your mind, and how it affected your behavior afterward.

This awareness becomes our starting point for understanding the nature of rejection and how it shapes our lives.

The Many Faces of Rejection

Rejection weaves through our lives in countless ways, each with its own particular sting.

In our professional lives, it might show up as a promotion that goes to someone else, or a proposal that falls flat in front of decision-makers. These moments can shake our confidence in our abilities and make us question our career path.

In our personal lives, rejection often cuts even deeper. A relationship ending, a friend growing distant, or family disapproval can make us question not just our choices but our very worth as individuals.

Even in our creative endeavors, where we pour our heart and soul into our work, rejection can feel like a direct challenge to our identity and potential.

Start noticing how rejection appears in different areas of your life. You might discover that you handle professional rejection differently than personal rejection, or that creative rejection triggers unique responses.

Understanding these patterns helps you develop more effective ways of responding to each type.

The Deep Roots of Rejection

Have you ever noticed how a single rejection can make you question everything about yourself? This happens because rejection taps into our fundamental need for belonging.

From an evolutionary standpoint, being accepted by our group wasn't just about feeling good—it was about survival itself. In today's world, we still carry this primitive wiring, which explains why even seemingly small rejections can trigger such profound responses.

When we face rejection, our brain doesn't just register the specific instance; it triggers a cascade of self-doubt. We might find ourselves thinking "Maybe I'm not good enough" or "Why does this always happen to me?"

This is why even minor rejections can feel overwhelming—they tap into our deepest insecurities about our place in the world.

Begin tracking these thoughts when rejection occurs. Notice how your mind tries to make sense of the experience and what stories it creates.

This awareness helps you recognize when you're catastrophizing a single rejection into a judgment about your entire worth.

Understanding Our Response Patterns

When rejection hits, our reactions often fall into predictable patterns. Some of us fight back, becoming defensive or trying desperately to prove our worth.

Others flee, withdrawing from opportunities and avoiding similar situations in the future. And some of us freeze, becoming paralyzed with self-doubt and unable to move forward.

Understanding your typical response pattern is crucial because it shapes how rejection affects your life long after the initial sting fades.

Many people find themselves holding back from opportunities, self-sabotaging before others can reject them, or setting smaller goals to avoid potential rejection.

These protective behaviors might feel safe in the moment, but they ultimately limit our potential for growth and connection.

For the next week, observe your natural response to any hint of rejection. Do you become combative? Do you withdraw? Do you shut down?

Writing about these patterns helps you recognize your automatic responses, giving you the power to choose different reactions.

The Path Forward

Here's what's important to understand: Rejection itself isn't the problem. It's a natural part of life that everyone faces. What matters is how we interpret and respond to it.

Every successful person you admire has faced rejection—probably more times than you realize. What sets them apart isn't an absence of rejection but their relationship with it.

Start viewing rejection as information rather than judgment. Each rejection can teach you something valuable about yourself, your goals, or your approach.

When you receive a "no," ask yourself: What can I learn from this experience? How might this redirect me toward something better aligned with my path?

Key Takeaways

1. Rejection affects us on physical, emotional, and psychological levels

2. Our response patterns to rejection develop early and run deep

3. Understanding our automatic reactions gives us choice

4. Everyone faces rejection—success lies in how we handle it

5. Rejection can become a tool for growth rather than a source of limitation

Your Call to Action: The Seven-Day Rejection Awareness Practice

This week, begin developing a new relationship with rejection through daily observation and reflection:

Day 1: Physical Awareness—Notice and document how rejection affects your body.

Day 2: Emotional Mapping—Track the feelings that arise when facing rejection.

Day 3: Thought Patterns—Observe the stories your mind creates about rejection.

Days 4-7: Response Integration—Practice viewing rejection as information rather than judgment, noting what you learn each time.

Remember: Understanding rejection is different from being controlled by it. The work we've begun in this chapter—recognizing rejection's impact and our responses to it—lays the foundation for all the transformation ahead.

Take time to really know your relationship with rejection. Your honest reflection now will guide your growth throughout this journey.

The path forward isn't about avoiding rejection—it's about transforming how you experience and use it.

As we continue, you'll discover that rejection, handled correctly, can become one of your most powerful tools for growth and self-discovery.

Chapter 2: The Science Behind Rejection

Have you ever wondered why a simple "no" can feel like a physical blow? Or why you can still remember, with perfect clarity, rejections that happened years ago?

The answer lies in the remarkable way our brains process rejection, and understanding this can transform how you handle these challenging moments.

When someone rejects us, our brain doesn't just register emotional discomfort—it triggers the same neural pathways that process physical pain.

This isn't just a poetic metaphor; it's a scientific reality that researchers have documented through brain imaging studies.

When you hear that someone doesn't want to hire you, or that special someone isn't interested, your brain responds as if you've been physically hurt.

Take a moment now to recall a recent rejection. Notice where you feel it in your body. This awareness of the mind-body connection becomes crucial for managing rejection more effectively.

Our Ancient Survival System

This intense reaction to rejection isn't a flaw in our design—it's a feature that helped our ancestors survive. Thousands of years ago, being rejected from our social group didn't just mean emotional discomfort; it could mean death.

Those who felt rejection most keenly were more likely to maintain their social bonds and survive to pass on their genes.

We are their descendants, carrying their heightened sensitivity to social rejection in our modern world.

Consider how this ancient programming plays out in your own life. When you face rejection, you might notice your heart racing, your palms sweating, or a knot forming in your stomach.

These physical responses are part of your body's threat detection system, preparing you to either fight for acceptance or flee from the painful situation.

It's the same system that would activate if you encountered a physical threat, which explains why rejection can feel so overwhelming.

Start keeping a physical response journal this week. Each time you experience rejection, even small ones, note your body's reactions.

This practice helps you recognize your personal rejection response pattern, making it easier to manage these reactions when they arise.

The Emotional Cascade

Understanding the cascade of emotions that follows rejection helps us navigate it more effectively. When rejection hits, our brains release stress hormones like cortisol, which can affect everything from our sleep patterns to our immune system.

This biological response can trigger a cycle of negative thoughts and emotions that, if left unchecked, can impact our mental and physical wellbeing.

But here's where knowledge becomes power: Once you understand that your brain is running an ancient survival program, you can begin to update your response.

You can learn to recognize these biological reactions for what they are—evolutionary echoes rather than accurate assessments of your worth or future potential.

Practice naming your body's reactions when rejection occurs: "This is cortisol flowing through my system" or "My ancient survival system is activated right now."

This simple act of naming helps engage your prefrontal cortex—the rational, problem-solving part of your brain—reducing the intensity of the emotional response.

The Role of Memory and Pattern Recognition

Our brains are remarkably efficient at storing and recalling rejection experiences. This is why one rejection can trigger memories of past rejections, creating what feels like an avalanche of negative experiences.

Your brain does this to protect you, but in our modern world, this heightened memory for rejection can create unnecessary suffering.

Consider how this plays out in everyday situations. When you're about to send an important email, pitch an idea, or express interest in someone, your brain quickly scans through its rejection archive, bringing up every similar situation that ended in disappointment. This isn't random cruelty—it's your brain trying to protect you from potential social pain.

Try keeping a "Rejection Memory Log" for a week. Notice when past rejections surface in your mind and what triggered these memories. Understanding these patterns helps you respond more consciously rather than reacting from fear.

Breaking the Cycle

The good news is that understanding the science of rejection gives us powerful tools for changing our relationship with it.

Just as our brains can be conditioned to fear rejection, they can be reconditioned to handle it more effectively. This isn't about suppressing our natural responses—it's about working with our biology rather than against it.

Each time you face rejection, practice what I call the "Pause and Name" technique. Pause to acknowledge what's happening in your body and brain. Name the physical sensations and emotional responses you're experiencing.

This simple practice helps create space between the trigger and your response, allowing you to choose how you react rather than being driven by automatic patterns.

The Path to Neural Rewiring

Research shows that our brains are remarkably adaptable, capable of forming new neural pathways throughout our lives. This means that each time you handle rejection in a new, more constructive way, you're literally rewiring your brain's response pattern.

It's a process called neuroplasticity, and it's the foundation for building lasting resilience.

Begin consciously creating new neural pathways by practicing small exposures to rejection. Start with low-stakes situations where rejection wouldn't be devastating.

Notice your responses, practice your new tools, and celebrate each time you handle rejection differently than before.

Key Takeaways

1. Your brain processes rejection as physical pain—this is normal and natural

2. Understanding your body's rejection response helps you recognize and manage it

3. Naming your physical and emotional responses reduces their power over you

4. Your brain can be retrained to handle rejection more effectively

5. Each time you face rejection consciously, you're building new neural pathways

Your Call to Action: The Seven-Day Brain Training Challenge

Each day this week, focus on one aspect of your rejection response:

Day 1: Physical Awareness—Notice and document bodily sensations related to rejection.

Day 2: Emotional Tracking—Map the emotional cascade that follows rejection.

Day 3: Memory Patterns—Notice when past rejections surface and what triggers them.

Days 4-7: Response Rewiring—Practice the Pause and Name technique with any rejection experiences.

Remember: Your brain's intense response to rejection isn't a weakness—it's a sign that you're human, equipped with the same survival mechanisms that helped our species thrive.

By understanding this biology, you can begin working with your brain rather than against it.

Chapter 3: Processing Rejection - From Pain to Growth

When rejection first hits, it's tempting to push past the pain as quickly as possible. Our natural instinct is to either tough it out or try to forget it happened.

But what if the way through rejection isn't about pushing past the pain, but about learning to process it in a way that leads to genuine growth?

Think of emotional processing like digestion—you can't rush it, and trying to skip steps only leads to problems later. Just as your body needs time to break down and absorb nutrients from food, your mind needs time to process and integrate rejection experiences.

Take a moment now to consider how you typically handle rejection. Do you try to push through quickly? Do you get stuck in the pain? Your awareness of your current pattern becomes the foundation for developing a healthier approach.

The Natural Stages of Processing

Understanding the natural stages of processing rejection helps us navigate them more effectively. While everyone's journey is unique, knowing these common phases can help you trust the process and give yourself the time and space needed for true integration.

The journey begins with Impact—that initial blow of rejection that often feels like a shock to our system. This is when our emotional and physical responses are strongest. Your heart might race, your mind might go blank, or you might feel a surge of emotions you can't quite name.

During this stage, your primary task is simply to acknowledge what's happening without trying to fix or change it. Try placing your hand on your heart and saying, "This is the impact. I'm feeling it now." This simple acknowledgment helps you stay present with the experience rather than fighting against it.

As the initial shock subsides, we enter the Recognition stage. This is when thoughts and emotions start to surface more clearly. You might find yourself replaying the situation, questioning what went wrong, or feeling waves of different emotions.

This stage is about becoming aware, and your task is to let yourself feel without judgment. Start keeping a recognition journal, noting the thoughts and feelings that arise without trying to change them. This practice helps you develop the capacity to stay present with difficult emotions.

The Integration stage follows, where we begin making sense of the experience. Rather than just feeling the rejection, we start to understand it in the context of our larger life story.

This stage often brings important insights about ourselves, our goals, and our patterns. Your task here is to stay curious about what this experience might be teaching you.

Write about your rejection experience from different perspectives—what might your future self understand about this moment that you can't see right now?

Next comes Meaning-Making, where we begin to find significance in the rejection. This doesn't mean pretending it was a good thing—it means understanding how this experience fits into your larger journey.

Maybe a job rejection helps clarify what you really want in your career, or a relationship ending helps you recognize patterns you need to address.

Take time to explore what meanings are emerging from your experience, writing about both the challenges and the potential opportunities you can now see.

Finally, we reach the Growth stage, where rejection becomes a catalyst for transformation. This is when you can take what you've learned and use it to make conscious choices about moving forward.

Your task here is to transform insights into action. Choose one learning from your rejection experience and create a specific plan for how you'll implement it in your life.

The Art of Sitting with Discomfort

One of the most challenging aspects of processing rejection is learning to sit with uncomfortable emotions without trying to escape them. This doesn't mean wallowing—it means creating space to feel what you feel while maintaining perspective.

Try this visualization: Imagine your emotions are like weather patterns passing through the sky of your mind. Just as you wouldn't try to fight the rain or push away clouds, you don't need to fight or push away your feelings about rejection. Your task is to observe them with curiosity while remembering that, like all weather, they will pass.

Practice this weather watching several times throughout your day. Notice what emotional weather patterns tend to arise around rejection. Some days might bring stormy emotions, others might feel more like a gentle rain. The key is remembering that all weather eventually passes.

Practical Tools for Growth

The Emotional Check-In becomes your daily practice for developing awareness. Set aside a few minutes each day to check in with yourself about how you're feeling.

Don't try to change anything—just notice. This simple practice helps you develop emotional awareness and prevents unexpressed feelings from building up.

Writing becomes another powerful tool for processing emotions. Try writing a letter expressing everything you feel about the rejection—knowing you'll never send it.

This gives you complete freedom to be honest without worrying about impact or consequences. Let your thoughts and feelings flow onto the page without censoring or editing.

When you're ready, explore The Growth Question: "What might this rejection be making possible?" Notice that this is different from forcing a positive spin.

It's about exploring possibilities while honoring your experience. Write about what doors might be opening, even as others have closed.

Common Processing Pitfalls

Many of us try to speed through emotional processing, thinking we should be "over it" by now. Remember:

Genuine processing takes time, and trying to rush it often means we'll need to revisit these feelings later. Give yourself permission to move at your own pace.

You might be tempted to jump straight to finding the silver lining without fully acknowledging your pain. But trying to skip stages of processing usually means they'll show up later in unexpected ways. Trust that each stage serves a purpose in your healing journey.

Sometimes we can get stuck in one stage, particularly if the rejection triggers old wounds.

If you notice yourself stuck in the same thoughts or feelings for an extended period, it might be time to seek support from a trusted friend or professional.

Key Takeaways

1. Processing rejection is a natural journey through distinct stages

2. Each stage serves a purpose and deserves attention

3. Rushing or skipping stages can prolong the impact of rejection

4. Supporting yourself through the process is crucial for growth

5. Processing rejection well builds resilience for future challenges

Your Call to Action: The Seven-Day Processing Practice

This week, commit to conscious processing through daily reflection. Each day, spend time with these prompts:

Day 1: Impact Awareness—Notice and document your initial responses to rejection.

Day 2: Emotional Recognition—Explore and name the feelings that arise.

Day 3: Integration Reflection—Consider how this experience connects to your larger story.

Days 4-7: Growth Exploration—Look for emerging meanings and possibilities while honoring your experience.

Remember: Processing rejection well isn't about getting rid of the pain—it's about transforming it into wisdom that serves your growth.

Trust the process, give yourself time, and watch as pain gradually transforms into understanding.

Chapter 4: Breaking Free from Social Conditioning

Imagine standing in front of a mirror, but the reflection you see isn't entirely your own. It's layered with expectations, beliefs, and stories that others have placed upon you throughout your life.

From our earliest days, we absorb messages about success, failure, and worth: "Play it safe." "Don't aim too high." "What will people think?"

These aren't just casual remarks—they're part of a complex web of social conditioning that shapes how we handle rejection and what we believe is possible for our lives.

Before we go further, pause and look at your own reflection. What messages do you see layered over your true self? Take a moment to write down the voices that echo in your mind when you face or anticipate rejection. This awareness becomes your starting point for transformation.

The Invisible Scripts That Guide Us

Social conditioning runs deeper than simple advice or occasional comments. It's a sophisticated system of beliefs that infiltrates every aspect of how we understand ourselves and our possibilities.

These scripts often sound like wisdom, passed down through generations with the best intentions. But they can also become invisible prison walls, limiting our potential and magnifying the sting of rejection.

Think about the last time you faced rejection. Beyond the immediate disappointment, what other voices chimed in?

Perhaps you heard echoes of past warnings: "I told you it was risky" or "This is what happens when you reach too high." These aren't your natural responses to rejection—they're learned interpretations, shaped by years of social conditioning.

Start noticing these voices this week. Write down the phrases that arise when you face or consider potential rejection. Where did these messages come from? Who first taught you to interpret rejection this way?

Understanding the Layers

Our relationship with rejection is first shaped by our families. Watch a child experience rejection, and you'll likely see them look to their parents or caregivers to understand how to respond.

These early patterns become our default templates for processing rejection throughout life. The child who sees their parent respond to setbacks with resilience learns one story; the child who witnesses shame or withdrawal learns another.

Think back to your earliest memories of rejection. How did the adults in your life handle their own rejections? How did they respond to yours?

Write about these memories, not to judge but to understand the patterns you inherited.

Cultural influences add another layer to our conditioning. Different cultures carry profoundly different messages about risk, success, and the meaning of rejection.

Some view rejection as a personal failure that brings shame to the family, while others see it as a natural part of growth and achievement.

Understanding your cultural inheritance around rejection helps you choose which aspects serve your growth and which might need questioning.

Modern society adds yet another layer of complexity. Social media showcases endless "overnight success" stories while hiding the countless rejections that preceded them.

This creates a distorted view where rejection feels like a personal failure rather than a natural part of any journey toward meaningful achievement.

The Cost of Unconscious Conditioning

When we operate from unconscious social conditioning, rejection becomes more than just a "no"—it becomes confirmation of our deepest fears and limiting beliefs.

We might find ourselves abandoning dreams because they don't fit others' expectations, avoiding opportunities because we've internalized messages about "staying in our lane," or taking rejection as proof that we shouldn't have tried in the first place.

Begin tracking the cost of your conditioning. For one week, notice moments when you hold back, play small, or avoid possibilities because of internalized messages about rejection. Write down what you didn't do and the belief that stopped you.

Breaking Free: The Path to Authentic Response

Liberation from social conditioning isn't about wholesale rejection of everything you've learned. Instead, it's about developing the capacity to discern which beliefs serve your growth and which limit your potential. This process begins with awareness and develops through conscious choice.

Start noticing the thoughts that arise when you face rejection. Which ones feel like your authentic voice, and which sound more like inherited beliefs? Pay particular attention to absolute statements like "This always happens" or "I should have known better."

For each limiting belief you identify, explore its origins: Where did this belief come from? Does it reflect your true values and aspirations? How might your life be different without this belief?

Write about these questions in your journal, allowing yourself to imagine new possibilities.

Creating New Patterns

Every time you face rejection with awareness of your conditioning, you have an opportunity to write a new story. Instead of automatically falling into inherited patterns, you can pause and choose how to interpret and respond to the experience.

Start practicing this pause. When rejection hits, take three deep breaths before responding. In that space, ask yourself: "Is this my truth, or is this my conditioning speaking?" This simple practice begins to break the automatic cycle of conditioned responses.

Key Takeaways

1. Social conditioning shapes our relationship with rejection from our earliest experiences

2. Our automated responses often come from inherited beliefs rather than personal truth

3. Awareness of our conditioning is the first step toward authentic responses

4. We can consciously choose which beliefs to keep and which to release

5. Creating new patterns requires consistent practice and patience

Your Call to Action: The Seven-Day Liberation Practice

Each day this week, focus on one aspect of breaking free from conditioning:

Day 1: Awareness—Notice and write down the conditioned responses that arise around rejection.

acceptance. When facing rejection, notice your immediate impulse.

Do you fight against reality, trying to force a different outcome? Do you deny your feelings, pushing them away? Or do you collapse into helplessness?

Write down what you observe. This awareness becomes your starting point for developing true acceptance.

Understanding True Acceptance

Acceptance isn't about liking what happened or pretending you're not disappointed. It's about acknowledging reality exactly as it is, without wasting energy fighting against what has already occurred.

This might sound simple, but it's one of the most powerful shifts you can make in your relationship with rejection.

When rejection hits, our first instinct is often to resist—to argue with reality, to prove the other person wrong, or to deny our feelings about what happened.

This resistance, while natural, keeps us stuck in the pain of rejection rather than allowing us to move through it. Notice how much energy you spend fighting against what has already happened.

Imagine what might be possible if you redirected that energy toward growth and forward movement.

The Three Levels of Acceptance

First comes factual acceptance— acknowledging the basic reality of what happened. For example, "I applied for the job, and they chose someone else." No stories, no interpretations—just the plain facts.

This level of acceptance is like acknowledging that it's raining. You might not like the rain, but denying its existence won't keep you dry.

Take a recent rejection and practice writing about it in purely factual terms. Notice how different this feels from your usual way of thinking about it. What changes when you strip away the interpretations and focus only on what actually happened?

The second level is emotional acceptance. This involves accepting your feelings about the rejection without judgment. All emotions are valid—disappointment, anger, sadness, relief, or even a mix of many feelings.

Emotional acceptance doesn't mean you want these feelings or that you'll feel them forever. It simply means you acknowledge them as part of your current experience.

Spend some time each day this week simply naming your emotions about rejection without trying to change them. "Right now, I'm feeling disappointed." "In this moment, there's anger." Notice how this simple acknowledgment often helps emotions flow rather than get stuck.

The deepest level is experiential acceptance. This involves understanding that this rejection is now part of your life experience. It has happened, and it contributes to your story.

This doesn't mean it defines you or determines your future—it simply means you accept it as one of many experiences that shape your journey.

The Paradox of Acceptance

Here's something that might surprise you: The moment you truly accept a rejection is often the moment you begin to move beyond it. This seems counterintuitive. Shouldn't accepting rejection mean you're stuck with it?

Actually, the opposite is true. When you stop fighting against what has already happened, you free up enormous amounts of energy that you can redirect toward growth and forward movement.

Think about times in your life when you finally accepted something you'd been resisting. What changed in that moment? How did it feel to stop fighting reality? What became possible once you accepted what was?

Creating Your Acceptance Practice

Begin each day this week with a simple acceptance check-in. Notice what you're currently resisting in your life. Take three deep breaths with each recognition: "This is what's happening right now." Feel how your body responds to this acknowledgment.

When you notice yourself fighting against rejection, try this visualization: Imagine your emotions are like weather patterns passing through the sky of your mind.

Just as you wouldn't try to fight the rain or push away clouds, you don't need to fight or push away your feelings about rejection. Your task is to observe them with curiosity while remembering that, like all weather, they will pass.

Moving from Acceptance to Growth

Once you've developed a foundation of acceptance, you can begin asking powerful questions: What can I learn from this experience? How might this redirect me toward something better aligned with my path? What strengths did I show in putting myself out there?

Write these questions in your journal and return to them regularly. Let them guide you from mere acceptance to active growth.

Key Takeaways

1. Acceptance is not endorsement—it's acknowledging reality as it is

2. Fighting reality drains energy that could be used for growth

Chapter 5: The Art of Acceptance

The word "acceptance" often gets misunderstood. When it comes to rejection, many people think acceptance means giving up, agreeing with the rejection, or admitting defeat.

But true acceptance is something entirely different—it's the foundation upon which all genuine transformation is built.

Think of acceptance like learning to swim. Fighting against the water only exhausts you and can pull you under. But when you learn to work with the water, to accept its presence and nature, you discover the ability to move through it with grace and purpose.

The same principle applies to rejection.

Before we go further, take a moment to explore your current relationship with

Day 2: Origin Stories—Explore where your key beliefs about rejection came from.

Day 3: Questioning Challenge—one inherited belief about rejection that limits you.

Days 4-7: Conscious Choice—Practice responding to situations from your authentic self rather than your conditioning.

Remember: Breaking free from social conditioning isn't about rejecting everything you've learned. It's about consciously choosing which beliefs align with your authentic self and support your growth.

Each time you pause to question an inherited belief, you create space for your true voice to emerge.

Key Takeaways

1. Social conditioning shapes our relationship with rejection from our earliest experiences

2. Our automated responses often come from inherited beliefs rather than personal truth

3. Awareness of our conditioning is the first step toward authentic responses

4. We can consciously choose which beliefs to keep and which to release

5. Creating new patterns requires consistent practice and patience

Your Call to Action: The Seven-Day Liberation Practice

Each day this week, focus on one aspect of breaking free from conditioning:

Day 1: Awareness—Notice and write down the conditioned responses that arise around rejection.

For each limiting belief you identify, explore its origins: Where did this belief come from? Does it reflect your true values and aspirations? How might your life be different without this belief?

Write about these questions in your journal, allowing yourself to imagine new possibilities.

Creating New Patterns

Every time you face rejection with awareness of your conditioning, you have an opportunity to write a new story. Instead of automatically falling into inherited patterns, you can pause and choose how to interpret and respond to the experience.

Start practicing this pause. When rejection hits, take three deep breaths before responding. In that space, ask yourself: "Is this my truth, or is this my conditioning speaking?" This simple practice begins to break the automatic cycle of conditioned responses.

Take a recent rejection and practice writing about it in purely factual terms. Notice how different this feels from your usual way of thinking about it. What changes when you strip away the interpretations and focus only on what actually happened?

The second level is emotional acceptance. This involves accepting your feelings about the rejection without judgment. All emotions are valid—disappointment, anger, sadness, relief, or even a mix of many feelings.

Emotional acceptance doesn't mean you want these feelings or that you'll feel them forever. It simply means you acknowledge them as part of your current experience.

Spend some time each day this week simply naming your emotions about rejection without trying to change them. "Right now, I'm feeling disappointed." "In this moment, there's anger." Notice how this simple acknowledgment often helps emotions flow rather than get stuck.

The deepest level is experiential acceptance. This involves understanding that this rejection is now part of your life experience. It has happened, and it contributes to your story.

This doesn't mean it defines you or determines your future—it simply means you accept it as one of many experiences that shape your journey.

The Paradox of Acceptance

Here's something that might surprise you: The moment you truly accept a rejection is often the moment you begin to move beyond it. This seems counterintuitive. Shouldn't accepting rejection mean you're stuck with it?

Actually, the opposite is true. When you stop fighting against what has already happened, you free up enormous acceptance. When facing rejection, notice your immediate impulse.

Do you fight against reality, trying to force a different outcome? Do you deny your feelings, pushing them away? Or do you collapse into helplessness?

Write down what you observe. This awareness becomes your starting point for developing true acceptance.

Understanding True Acceptance

Acceptance isn't about liking what happened or pretending you're not disappointed. It's about acknowledging reality exactly as it is, without wasting energy fighting against what has already occurred.

This might sound simple, but it's one of the most powerful shifts you can make in your relationship with rejection.

When rejection hits, our first instinct is often to resist—to argue with reality, to prove the other person wrong, or to deny our feelings about what happened.

This resistance, while natural, keeps us stuck in the pain of rejection rather than allowing us to move through it. Notice how much energy you spend fighting against what has already happened.

Imagine what might be possible if you redirected that energy toward growth and forward movement.

The Three Levels of Acceptance

First comes factual acceptance—acknowledging the basic reality of what happened. For example, "I applied for the job, and they chose someone else." No stories, no interpretations—just the plain facts.

This level of acceptance is like acknowledging that it's raining. You might not like the rain, but denying its existence won't keep you dry.

3. True acceptance happens in stages and takes practice

4. Acceptance creates the foundation for meaningful change

5. You can accept a situation while still working to create different outcomes

Your Call to Action: The Seven-Day Acceptance Journey

Each day this week, commit to deepening your practice of acceptance:

Day 1: Focus on factual acceptance, stripping away interpretations from one situation.

Day 2: Practice emotional acceptance, allowing yourself to feel without judgment.

Day 3: Explore experiential acceptance, seeing how this moment fits into your larger story.

Days 4-7: Integrate all three levels of acceptance in your daily experiences, noting what you discover.

Remember: Acceptance isn't about giving up your power—it's about reclaiming it by choosing where to focus your energy.

When you accept what is, you create space for what could be.

Chapter 6: Building Resilience Through Practice

Most people think of resilience as something you either have or you don't—like it's a character trait you're born with.

But the truth is, resilience is more like a muscle. It grows stronger through deliberate practice and strategic challenges.

Just as an athlete doesn't become strong by thinking about weightlifting, you don't become resilient by simply understanding rejection. You need to actively engage with it.

Begin today by choosing one small action that carries the possibility of rejection—perhaps asking for something you normally wouldn't, or sharing an idea you might usually keep to yourself.

Notice how it feels before, during, and after. This becomes your first rep in building your resilience muscle.

Redefining Resilience

Let's start by clearing up a common misconception: Resilience isn't about becoming invulnerable to rejection or learning to "tough it out."

True resilience is about developing the flexibility to bounce back from setbacks and the wisdom to learn from them. It's not about hardening yourself—it's about becoming more adaptable.

Think of resilience like a tree in the wind. The strongest trees aren't the most rigid; they're the ones that can bend without breaking. They yield to the force of the wind while staying firmly rooted. This is the kind of resilience we're aiming to build.

Spend a few minutes today observing a tree moving in the wind. Notice how it bends and sways while maintaining its ground.

Write about how this metaphor applies to your own experience with rejection. When have you been too rigid? When have you found the strength to bend without breaking?

The Three Elements of Rejection Resilience

First comes emotional agility—the ability to experience rejection without being overwhelmed by it. This means developing the capacity to feel your emotions fully while maintaining your sense of self.

Start noticing your emotional responses to rejection without immediately trying to change them. Set three random alarms throughout your day. When they sound, take thirty seconds to notice and name your current emotional state without trying to shift it.

Next is strategic perspective—the ability to see rejection in its proper context. A resilient person can acknowledge the pain of rejection while recognizing it as one moment in a larger journey. They can separate the event of rejection from their sense of self-worth.

Practice this by drawing three concentric circles. In the center, write a recent rejection.

In the middle circle, list three possible opportunities this rejection might create.

In the outer circle, write how this might serve your growth in the long term.

Finally, there's recovery capacity—the ability to process rejection in a way that makes you stronger rather than more fragile. This isn't just about how quickly you bounce back—it's about how effectively you integrate the experience.

After your next rejection, set a timer for 24 hours. During this time, notice and document your recovery process. What helps you bounce back? What slows your recovery?

Building Your Practice

Just as an athlete follows a training program, building rejection resilience requires a systematic approach. Start with low-stakes situations where rejection is possible but not devastating.

Perhaps it's asking for a small discount at a store, making a suggestion in a meeting, or reaching out to connect with someone new. The goal isn't to succeed or fail—it's to build your comfort with the possibility of rejection.

Create your own "Rejection Resilience Workout Plan" for the week. Each day, choose one small action that stretches your comfort zone slightly.

Track your experiences like you would track physical exercises, noting both the challenge and your response to it.

The Power of Small Wins

Building resilience isn't about dramatic transformations—it's about accumulating small wins that gradually expand your comfort zone.

Each time you face a potential rejection and survive, regardless of the outcome, you're building evidence that rejection is survivable.

Start keeping what I call a "Victory Vault"—a special place where you record each time you face rejection and survive.

Write down not just what happened, but what you learned about yourself in the process. This becomes your personal evidence bank of resilience, something you can return to when facing bigger challenges.

Creating Your Recovery Ritual

Developing a personal recovery ritual is crucial for building resilience. This is your go-to process for bouncing back from rejection.

Start by acknowledging the impact—name the rejection, recognize your feelings, honor your effort. Then extract the learning—what worked well, what could you adjust, what surprised you?

Finally, reset and redirect—reconnect with your goals, identify next steps, take one small action.

Practice your recovery ritual with small disappointments to make it automatic for bigger rejections. The more familiar this process becomes, the more naturally you'll implement it when you need it most.

Visualizing Growth

Just as athletes use visualization to improve performance, you can use it to build rejection resilience. Spend a few minutes each day imagining yourself handling rejection with grace and wisdom.

See yourself implementing your recovery ritual and emerging stronger. Make this visualization practice part of your morning routine, setting the tone for resilient responses throughout your day.

Key Takeaways

1. Resilience is a skill that develops through consistent practice

2. Small, regular exposure to rejection builds capacity for bigger challenges

3. Recovery rituals are essential for building lasting resilience

4. Progress comes through accumulated small wins

5. Visualization strengthens resilient responses

Your Call to Action: The Seven-Day Resilience Challenge

Day 1: Begin with Awareness—Notice and document how you typically respond to rejection, creating your baseline for growth.

Day 2: Strategic Exposure—Choose one small rejection possibility to face deliberately, focusing on your response rather than the outcome.

Day 3: Recovery Practice—Implement your recovery ritual after any setbacks, no matter how small.

Day 4: Perspective Building—Practice seeing rejection through the lens of growth, documenting potential opportunities in each challenge.

Days 5-7: Integration—Combine all you've learned, gradually increasing the challenge level while maintaining your recovery practices.

Remember: True resilience isn't about never falling—it's about learning to rise again with greater wisdom each time.

Start small, stay consistent, and watch your resilience grow through deliberate practice.

Chapter 7: The Art of Authentic Connection After Rejection

When rejection strikes, our natural instinct is often to withdraw. We build invisible walls, hold people at arm's length, and protect ourselves from potential future pain.

While this protective response makes perfect sense, it creates an ironic problem: the very time we most need meaningful connection is precisely when we're most likely to push it away.

Think about the last time you faced rejection. Perhaps you stopped sharing your goals to avoid having to share potential failures. Maybe you became more guarded in relationships to prevent future hurt.

While these protective measures might feel safe in the moment, they often lead to a kind of self-imposed isolation that can be more painful than the rejection itself.

The Connection Paradox

Here's the challenging truth about rejection: it often makes us feel isolated precisely when connection could help us most.

We withdraw to protect ourselves, but in doing so, we cut ourselves off from one of our most powerful sources of resilience—authentic human connection.

This withdrawal might feel like putting on armor, but it's armor that weighs us down and keeps us from the very experiences that could help us heal.

Take a moment now to notice your current connection patterns. Are you holding back from sharing your experiences? Have you been declining invitations or avoiding social situations?

Write down three ways you might be protecting yourself from connection right now. This awareness becomes your starting point for change.

Understanding the Withdrawal Response

Our tendency to withdraw after rejection makes perfect evolutionary sense. Just as our ancestors learned to avoid physical pain by pulling back from fire, we learn to avoid emotional pain by pulling back from potential rejection.

But here's the crucial difference: while avoiding fire is always smart, avoiding connection because of past rejection often means missing opportunities for growth and support.

The next time you notice yourself pulling back from connection, pause for a moment. Feel the impulse to withdraw, but don't act on it immediately.

Instead, write down what you're protecting yourself from and what you might be missing by withdrawing. This simple practice helps you make more conscious choices about connection.

Creating Authentic Connection

Authentic connection isn't about collecting friends or networking contacts. It's about creating genuine relationships where you can be yourself—including the parts that feel vulnerable or uncertain.

This kind of connection serves as both a buffer against rejection's sting and a foundation for greater resilience.

Start small in building these connections. Choose one person you trust and share something slightly vulnerable—perhaps a hope you have or a challenge you're facing.

Notice how it feels to be genuine with another person. Pay attention to both the fear and the potential for deeper connection.

The Building Blocks of Connection

Authentic connection grows through several essential elements. First is mutual vulnerability—the willingness to be seen and to truly see others.

Next comes genuine interest in each other's experiences, not just waiting for your turn to speak.

Then there's the ability to share both successes and struggles, creating a full picture of your human experience.

Finally, there's the space for both people to be their true selves, without pressure to perform or pretend.

Choose one of these elements to practice each day this week. Notice how focusing on just one aspect of connection at a time makes the process feel more manageable and authentic.

Breaking the Isolation Cycle

Moving from withdrawal to connection requires conscious effort and patience. Begin by checking in with yourself. What are you really feeling? What kind of support would feel meaningful right now?

This self-awareness helps you connect with others from a place of authenticity rather than need.

Create a simple connection practice for yourself. Each day, choose one small way to reach out to someone else.

It might be sending a thoughtful message, sharing an insight, or simply asking how they're doing and really listening to their response. Notice how these small connections begin to create a web of support around you.

The Power of Shared Experience

One of the most powerful ways to build authentic connection is through shared experiences of challenge and growth.

When you're willing to be honest about your rejections and what you're learning from them, you create space for others to do the same. This shared vulnerability often leads to deeper, more meaningful connections.

Try this: The next time someone shares a struggle with you, resist the urge to immediately offer advice or fix their problem.

Instead, simply acknowledge their experience and share a time when you felt something similar. Notice how this kind of sharing creates a different quality of connection.

Key Takeaways

1. Withdrawal after rejection is natural but often counterproductive

2. Authentic connection builds resilience against future rejection

3. Small, consistent steps toward connection create lasting change

4. Shared vulnerability strengthens relationships

5. Regular connection practices build emotional resilience

Your Call to Action: The Seven-Day Connection Challenge

Over the next week, commit to rebuilding authentic connection in your life. Each day focuses on a different aspect of connection:

Day 1: Self-Connection—Spend time writing about what authentic connection means to you and what might be holding you back.

Day 2: Safe Reopening—Choose one trusted person and share something meaningful about your current journey.

Day 3: Listening Deeply—In your conversations today, focus entirely on understanding others rather than being understood.

Day 4: Vulnerability Practice—Share one challenge you're facing with someone who has earned the right to hear it.

Days 5-7: Integration—Combine what you've learned about connection to create genuine interactions each day, noting what works best for you.

Remember: Building authentic connection isn't about being perfect—it's about being real.

Start where you are, with the people already in your life, and watch how small acts of authentic sharing can transform your relationship with both rejection and connection.

Chapter 8: Transforming Professional Identity After Rejection

Professional rejection cuts deeper than most other forms of rejection because it challenges not just what we do, but who we believe we are.

When you don't get that job you wanted, when you're passed over for a promotion, or when your ideas are dismissed in a meeting, it can shake the very foundation of how you see yourself.

For many of us, our professional identity has become so intertwined with our sense of self-worth that untangling the two feels nearly impossible.

Take a moment to reflect on your most recent professional rejection. Notice how it affected not just your mood or confidence in the moment, but your entire sense of professional self. This awareness becomes our starting point for transformation.

The Professional-Personal Identity Collision

That promotion you didn't get wasn't just about a title or salary—it represented validation of your skills, recognition of your worth, and confirmation of your career trajectory.

When it doesn't materialize, the rejection can trigger profound questions about your professional identity: "Am I really cut out for this field?" "Do I have what it takes?" "Should I have chosen a different path?"

These aren't just fleeting doubts. They're deep questions about who we are and who we're becoming professionally. The key to handling them lies in understanding the different layers of professional rejection and how each affects our sense of self.

Understanding the Layers

Professional rejection operates on multiple levels, and understanding each helps us respond more effectively. When you experience professional rejection, pause to examine which layer is most affected:

The Performance Layer: This is about specific actions or outcomes. Perhaps your presentation didn't land well, or your project didn't meet expectations. Remember, a single performance doesn't define your professional worth.

The Potential Layer: This touches on your future possibilities. A rejection might make you question your career trajectory or potential for growth. Yet potential isn't fixed—it's constantly evolving through experience and learning.

The Identity Layer: This deepest layer affects how you see yourself as a professional. It's where rejection can most powerfully impact your sense of self. Learning to protect and strengthen this layer becomes crucial for long-term resilience.

Start noting which layer each professional rejection affects most strongly. This awareness helps you respond more precisely and effectively to each setback.

Rebuilding Your Professional Foundation

Professional confidence isn't about never experiencing doubt—it's about knowing how to rebuild after setbacks. Begin by creating what I call an "Evidence Journal."

Each day, write down one piece of evidence of your professional capability. It might be positive feedback you received, a challenge you overcame, or a skill you demonstrated. This isn't about ego—it's about maintaining an accurate picture of your professional worth.

When professional rejection strikes, turn to this journal. Let it remind you that your worth isn't determined by a single outcome or another person's decision. Your capabilities exist independently of whether they're recognized in any given moment.

The Skill-Building Response

Transform rejection into a catalyst for growth by approaching it with curiosity rather than judgment.

After each professional setback, ask yourself: "What skill could I develop to be even stronger next time?" Then create a specific plan to develop that skill.

This approach shifts your focus from the pain of rejection to the possibility of growth. It gives you back a sense of control and direction, crucial elements for maintaining professional confidence.

Crafting Your Professional Narrative

The stories we tell about our professional journey shape not just how others see us, but how we see ourselves. After rejection, consciously reshape your professional narrative.

Instead of viewing rejections as failures, frame them as pivotal moments that directed you toward better alignment with your true professional path.

Write your professional story three times: once focusing on challenges, once on opportunities, and once on growth.

Notice how each version feels different and choose consciously which elements to emphasize in your ongoing narrative.

Learning from Feedback Without Internalizing Failure

Professional feedback can be valuable without becoming a judgment on your worth. Create what I call a "Feedback Filter System."

When receiving professional feedback, first write it down exactly as received. Then rewrite it in purely objective, actionable terms. This helps separate useful insights from emotional judgment.

Practice this translation process regularly, turning critical feedback into specific action steps while leaving your professional identity intact.

Redefining Professional Success

Perhaps the most powerful transformation comes from reconsidering what professional success really means to you.

Take time to explore questions like: *What truly matters to me in my professional life? How do I want to measure my success beyond titles and salary? What kind of impact do I want to have in my field?*

Write your answers, then revisit them after each significant professional experience, whether perceived as success or failure. Let your definition of success evolve as you grow.

Creating Your Professional Resilience Practice

Develop a daily practice to strengthen your professional identity. Each morning, set an intention for how you'll show up professionally, regardless of external recognition.

Each evening, acknowledge one way you honored your professional values or demonstrated your capabilities.

Remember, your professional identity isn't defined by any single outcome or another person's decision. It's built through consistent alignment with your values and continuous growth through both successes and setbacks.

Key Takeaways

1. Professional rejection affects both career path and personal identity

2. External outcomes don't define your professional worth

3. Building evidence of capability maintains perspective during setbacks

4. Feedback can inform growth without determining identity

5. Professional resilience grows stronger through conscious practice

Your Call to Action: The Professional Identity Strengthening Week

Over the next seven days, commit to strengthening your professional identity through daily practice:

Day 1: Professional Values—Clarity Write down your core professional values and one way you'll express each today.

Day 2: Capability Evidence—Document three significant professional challenges you've overcome and what each reveals about your capabilities.

Day 3: Feedback Translation—Take one piece of critical feedback and translate it into specific, actionable steps.

Day 4: Success Definition—Write your personal definition of meaningful professional success.

Days 5-7: Integration Practice—Each day, choose one aspect of your professional identity to strengthen through conscious action.

Remember: Your professional identity is bigger than any rejection or setback. It's shaped by every experience, lesson, and challenge you've faced.

Use rejection as a catalyst for growth rather than a limitation on your potential.

Chapter 9: Strengthening Personal Boundaries

The fear of rejection often leads us to have fuzzy boundaries.

Like a fence that's fallen into disrepair, we let others cross lines we've drawn, take on burdens that aren't ours to carry, and accept treatment that doesn't align with our values—all to avoid the possibility of rejection.

Yet here lies one of life's great paradoxes: weak boundaries actually make rejection hurt more, while strong boundaries help us build genuine resilience.

Take a moment right now to reflect on your past week. Notice how many times you said yes when your heart whispered no.

Write down each instance where you took on responsibilities that weren't yours, stayed in situations that drained you, or accepted treatment that felt wrong. These moments are your compass, pointing toward boundaries that need strengthening.

Understanding the Boundary-Rejection Connection

Think of boundaries like the walls of your home. They don't exist to imprison you or keep everyone out, but rather to create a safe space where you can choose who to let in and under what circumstances.

When rejection causes us to blur these boundaries, we end up compromising our wellbeing in ways that make us more vulnerable to future rejection.

Start observing how your boundaries shift when rejection feels close. *Do you work late to prove your worth? Do you go along with plans you don't enjoy to maintain friendships? Do you take on extra projects to avoid being seen as difficult?*

Each of these moments represents a boundary being crossed in response to fear.

The Cost of Compromised Boundaries

When we fear rejection, we often override our inner wisdom. We might find ourselves agreeing to things we don't want to do, shouldering others' responsibilities to prove our worth, or accepting disrespect to maintain relationships.

Each time we do this, we send ourselves a powerful message that avoiding rejection matters more than honoring our own needs and values.

Begin tracking the energy cost of weak boundaries. After each interaction where you compromise your boundaries, note your energy level, emotional state, and physical sensations. This awareness helps you recognize the true price of saying yes when you mean no.

Creating Strong Foundations

Strong boundaries aren't about building walls—they're about creating clear, healthy limits that allow for genuine connection while protecting your wellbeing. Start by exploring your core values and non-negotiables.

What treatment will you no longer accept? What commitments truly deserve your energy? What values must you honor to maintain your integrity?

Write about these questions in detail. Your answers become the foundation for stronger boundaries.

Remember: setting boundaries isn't selfish—it's creating conditions for sustainable giving and authentic connection.

The Art of Clear Communication

Setting boundaries effectively requires both clarity and skill. You don't need anger or defensiveness to maintain strong boundaries. Practice phrases like "I need to check my calendar before committing" or "That doesn't work for me right now." Notice how these statements are both clear and kind.

Record yourself saying these phrases. Listen to your tone. Practice until they feel as natural as saying hello. The more comfortable you become with boundary-setting language, the more readily you'll use it when needed.

Professional Boundaries

In the workplace, boundaries often feel especially challenging. Start with one area where lines feel fuzzy—perhaps it's checking email after hours or taking on tasks outside your role.

Create specific guidelines for yourself, like "No work emails after 7 PM" or "I'll review additional requests weekly rather than saying yes immediately."

Personal Boundaries

Personal relationships often present the greatest boundary challenges because they carry emotional weight. Begin with small boundaries in safe relationships.

Maybe it's taking time alone when you need it or not answering calls during dinner. Each successful boundary builds confidence for bigger ones.

Digital Boundaries

In our constantly connected world, digital boundaries become increasingly crucial. Set specific times for checking messages and stick to them.

Create notification-free zones in your day. Remember that your peace of mind matters more than instant responsiveness.

Navigating Resistance

When you start setting boundaries, expect some pushback. People in your life have grown accustomed to your previous patterns. Their resistance often indicates that your boundaries are necessary, not that you should abandon them. Stay gentle but firm in your new limits.

The Power of Consistent Practice

Think of boundary-setting like building muscle. Start with smaller weights— minor boundaries in safe situations.

Gradually increase the challenge as you build strength. Celebrate each time you maintain a boundary, no matter how small it seems.

Key Takeaways

1. Strong boundaries protect against future rejection

2. Clear limits create space for authentic connection

3. Setting boundaries requires practice and patience

4. Resistance to boundaries often confirms their necessity

5. Consistent boundary maintenance builds lasting resilience

Your Call to Action: The Seven-Day Boundary Revolution

Transform your relationship with boundaries through daily practice:

Day 1: Boundary Awareness—Document where your current boundaries feel weak or non-existent.

Day 2: Value Exploration—Write extensively about what truly matters to you and needs protection.

Day 3: Communication Practice—Record and practice boundary-setting phrases until they feel natural.

Days 4-7: Active Implementation—Choose one boundary each day to establish or strengthen, documenting your experience and insights.

Remember: Strong boundaries aren't walls—they're bridges to more authentic connections.

When you honor your boundaries, you teach others how to respect them too. Each time you maintain a healthy limit, you build greater resilience against rejection while creating space for more meaningful relationships.

Chapter 10: Identifying and Overcoming Lies

When rejection strikes, our minds become masterful storytellers, weaving narratives that feel absolutely true in the moment but actually hold us back from growth and resilience.

These stories—or lies, as we'll call them—can become so familiar that we stop questioning them. They whisper things like "You're not good enough," "This always happens to you," or "You'll never succeed."

Before we proceed further, take a moment to reflect on your most recent rejection. Notice the story your mind immediately created about it.

Write it down, exactly as your inner voice tells it. This becomes our starting point for uncovering the lies we've been believing.

The Purpose Behind the Lies

Our minds create these stories for a reason—they're trying to make sense of rejection and protect us from future pain. It's a natural and even loving impulse, but these protective stories often become self-fulfilling prophecies.

When we believe we're not good enough, we act from that belief, creating evidence that seems to confirm it.

Think of your mind as an overprotective parent. Just as a parent might try to discourage their child from trying something risky to prevent potential hurt, your mind creates these stories to protect you from future rejection.

Understanding this protective intention helps us approach these lies with compassion rather than judgment.

The Universal Lies

Certain lies about rejection appear so frequently they might be considered universal. The Permanence Lie tells us "I'll always face rejection" or "Nothing ever works out for me."

This lie turns temporary situations into permanent judgments, coloring our entire view of the future.

The Personality Lie whispers "There must be something wrong with me" or "I'm not the kind of person who succeeds." This lie transforms specific situations into character judgments, making rejection feel deeply personal and unchangeable.

The Pattern Lie convinces us that "This always happens to me" or "I'm just unlucky." This lie creates false patterns, making us hyperaware of rejections while overlooking successes and opportunities.

The Truth-Finding Framework

Finding truth amidst these lies requires patience and practice. Begin with one limiting belief that frequently arises after rejection. Write it down.

Now, treat it like a scientific hypothesis rather than an absolute truth. What actual evidence supports this belief? What evidence contradicts it? Are you confusing feelings with facts?

Spend time examining this belief from different angles. Imagine you're a detective gathering evidence both for and against it.

Write down everything you discover. Often, just this process of investigation begins to loosen the lie's hold on us.

Breaking the Lie-Behavior Loop

Our lies create a self-perpetuating cycle: We experience rejection, believe a lie about it, act based on that lie, create situations that seem to confirm the lie, and strengthen our belief in it. Breaking this cycle requires conscious intervention at any point.

Start tracking your lie-behavior loop. Notice when a rejection triggers a familiar lie, and pause before acting on it.

Take three deep breaths and ask yourself: "What would I do in this situation if I didn't believe this thought?" This creates space between the lie and your response to it.

Building Truth Resilience

Think of truth resilience like building immunity. Just as your body becomes stronger through exposure to small challenges, your mind becomes more resilient through regular practice with truth.

Each time you catch yourself believing a lie about rejection, pause and question it: "Is this thought helpful? Is it based on facts? Would I say this to a friend?"

Create a daily truth check-in practice. Each morning, write down one lie you're prone to believing. Beneath it, write a more balanced truth. Carry this truth with you throughout the day, returning to it whenever the lie surfaces.

The Power of New Narratives

As you become more skilled at identifying lies, you can begin creating new, more empowering narratives. These aren't about forced positivity—they're about finding balanced truth that serves your growth.

When rejection occurs, try writing three different interpretations of what happened. Notice how each version feels in your body. Which one supports your growth while honoring your experience?

Key Takeaways

1. Our minds create protective lies to shield us from future pain

2. These lies can become self-fulfilling prophecies if left unchallenged

3. Truth-finding is a skill that develops with practice

4. Evidence collection helps combat common lies

5. Building truth resilience requires consistent practice

Your Call to Action: The Seven-Day Truth Challenge

Each day this week, dedicate yourself to uncovering and transforming one rejection-related lie:

Day 1: Lie Detection—Notice and document the lies that arise when you think about rejection.

Day 2: Origin Stories—Explore where these lies first took root in your life.

Day 3: Evidence Gathering—Collect facts that challenge your most persistent lie.

Days 4-7: Truth Creation—Practice creating new, balanced narratives about rejection.

Remember: The lies rejection tells us are often our mind's misguided attempt at protection.

By learning to identify and challenge these lies with compassion and curiosity, we free ourselves to respond to rejection from a place of truth and possibility rather than fear and limitation.

Chapter 11: Owning Your Story

Every rejection you've faced is part of your story, but it doesn't have to be the story that defines you.

The power of personal narrative lies not in what happens to us, but in how we choose to tell our story.

When we learn to own our story—including the rejections, setbacks, and challenges—we transform from being characters in someone else's narrative to becoming the authors of our own experience.

Before we go further, take a moment to reflect on how you currently tell the story of your rejections. Do you cast yourself as the victim? The failure? The almost-made-it?

Write down your current narrative without editing or judgment. The way you frame your story shapes not only how others see you but, more importantly, how you see yourself and what you believe is possible for your future.

The Art of Story Structure

Every powerful story has natural elements that give it shape and meaning. Think about your recent rejection experience. What was happening in your life when this rejection occurred?

This is your context—not just the event itself, but the larger picture of who you were becoming at that time. Write about this moment, capturing both the outer circumstances and your inner landscape.

Now consider the challenge itself—the rejection you faced. Rather than seeing it as just a setback, try viewing it as a plot point in your larger story.

What makes this moment significant? How did it test you? Write about this challenge as if you're crafting a scene in a compelling narrative.

Next, explore the choice point—that moment when you decided how to respond to the rejection. This is where you begin to take control of your narrative.

Even if you wish you'd responded differently, write about what this choice revealed about you. What strengths or growing edges did it illuminate?

Finally, consider the change this experience created in you. How did this rejection serve as a catalyst? What shifted in your understanding, your approach, or your sense of self? Write about this transformation, however subtle it might have been.

Transforming Your Narrative

Let's practice transforming how you tell your rejection stories. Choose a recent rejection that still carries some emotional charge.

First, write it as you've been telling it. Then, let's shift the perspective. Instead of "I failed to get the promotion," try, "I had the courage to put myself forward for a challenging opportunity."

Rather than "They didn't want me," explore "This opened the door for something better aligned with my path."

Spend some time with these different versions of your story. Notice how each one feels in your body. *Which version energizes you? Which one creates space for growth?*

This isn't about forcing positivity—it's about finding a truth that serves your development while honoring your experience.

Becoming the Author

Before you can rewrite your story, you need to recognize how you're currently telling it. For the next three days, pay attention to your rejection narrative.

Notice the words you habitually use, the role you assign yourself, and the meaning you've attached to your experiences. Journal about these patterns each evening, becoming aware of the stories that have been running on autopilot.

As you gain awareness of your current narrative, begin looking for themes. *Do you tend to blame yourself? Do you see rejection as a permanent mark or a temporary redirect? Do you focus more on what you lost or what you learned?*

Understanding these patterns helps you choose more consciously how you want to tell your story going forward.

Crafting Your New Narrative

Now it's time to choose what role you want to play in your own story. Perhaps you're the learner, constantly growing through experience. Maybe you're the pioneer, blazing new trails despite setbacks.

Or you might be the phoenix, rising stronger from each challenge. Spend some time exploring different roles, trying them on like costumes until you find one that feels authentically yours.

Take one significant rejection and look at it through your chosen role. *What strengths did this experience reveal that you hadn't noticed before? What wisdom did you gain? How did this redirect you toward something better?*

Write this version of your story, allowing your new role to illuminate different aspects of the experience.

The Art of Integration

Creating a new narrative isn't just about rewriting one event—it's about weaving all your experiences into a coherent story of growth. Take time this week to create a timeline of significant rejections in your life.

For each one, note what it taught you, how you grew, and any unexpected positive outcomes that emerged. Look for patterns and connections between experiences. What larger story are these events telling?

Try writing letters between different versions of yourself—from your past self to your present self, from your present self to your future self.

What wisdom would each version share? What perspectives might they offer about the rejections you've faced? Let these different viewpoints enrich your understanding of your journey.

Finding Your Voice

As you become more comfortable with your story, practice telling it in different ways. Start with writing it just for yourself. Then perhaps share a small part with someone you trust.

Notice how the story evolves as you tell it, what details emerge as significant, what meanings become clearer through the telling.

Remember that you don't have to share every detail of your story with everyone. Part of owning your narrative is choosing what to share, when, and with whom.

Practice discerning what parts of your story might inspire others while maintaining healthy boundaries around your experience.

Your Next Step

This week, commit to one simple practice: Each evening, write about your day from the perspective of your chosen role—the learner, the pioneer, the phoenix.

Notice how this viewpoint changes how you interpret and integrate your experiences, especially any rejections or setbacks.

Key Takeaways

Throughout this chapter, we've explored several crucial insights about owning your story:

1. You are the author of your own narrative, with the power to shape how you tell your story

2. Every rejection can be reframed as part of a larger journey of growth

3. The way you tell your story shapes not just your past, but your future possibilities

4. Owning your story builds both resilience and authentic confidence

5. Your transformed narrative can inspire others while honoring your own journey

Your Call to Action: The Seven-Day Story Transformation

For the coming week, embark on a journey to transform your rejection narrative. Each day builds upon the previous one, creating a complete story transformation:

Day 1: Story Awareness—Begin by spending thirty minutes writing your current rejection story exactly as you see it. Don't edit or judge—just let it flow. Notice the themes, words, and emotions that emerge.

Day 2: Role Exploration—Take time today to explore different roles you might play in your story. Write three short versions of the same rejection event—as a learner, a pioneer, and a phoenix. Which resonates most deeply?

Day 3: Timeline Creation—Create your rejection-to-growth timeline. Start with your earliest remembered rejection and trace your journey to now, noting key moments of both challenge and transformation.

Day 4: Perspective Shift—Choose your most challenging rejection and write it from three different time perspectives: from the heat of the moment, from your current vantage point, and from your imagined future self five years ahead.

Day 5: Integration—Begin weaving your individual rejection stories into a larger narrative of growth. How does each experience connect to the others? What larger pattern emerges?

Days 6-7: Practice and Refinement—Spend these days practicing telling your new story. Write it, speak it aloud, share parts of it with trusted friends. Notice how it feels different in your body and how it opens new possibilities for your future.

Remember: Your story is yours to tell. By owning it fully—including the rejections and setbacks—you reclaim your power and create a narrative that serves your growth rather than limits it.

Each time you tell your story with intention, you strengthen your ability to create meaning from challenge and possibility from rejection.

Chapter 12: Moving Forward with Purpose

Rejection often feels like an ending, but it can actually be a powerful beginning.

When a door closes—whether it's a job opportunity, a relationship, or a creative project—we have a unique opportunity to pause and reassess our direction. In these moments of forced reflection, we often discover clarity about what truly matters to us.

Think about your most recent significant rejection. Beyond the immediate disappointment, did you notice how it pushed you to think more deeply about what you really wanted?

Sometimes it takes hearing "no" to understand what we genuinely want to say "yes" to. Rejection has a remarkable way of stripping away the non-essential and revealing what truly matters in our lives.

Finding Your True North

The time after rejection is perfect for deeper reflection. Instead of rushing to the next opportunity or relationship, take time to explore what truly matters to you.

This isn't about creating elaborate plans or setting ambitious goals—it's about connecting with your authentic desires and values.

Consider what you would pursue even if rejection was guaranteed. This question cuts through our fear of failure and connects us with what truly matters.

When we're honest with ourselves, we often discover that our deepest aspirations have nothing to do with avoiding rejection and everything to do with creating meaningful impact.

Write about what energizes you naturally. What makes you lose track of time? What would you regret not trying? These questions help reveal your natural inclinations and genuine interests. When we move in alignment with these authentic desires, rejection becomes less threatening because we're guided by something stronger than fear of failure.

The Purpose-Finding Process

Moving forward with purpose means making choices that reflect your values rather than your fears. Begin by examining your current direction.

Are you pursuing certain paths mainly to avoid rejection? Are there dreams you've abandoned out of fear?

Write about these questions honestly, allowing yourself to imagine what might be possible if fear of rejection wasn't holding you back.

Create what I call a "Purpose Map." Draw three concentric circles. In the innermost circle, write what you feel absolutely certain about regarding your purpose.

In the middle circle, write what you're exploring or curious about. In the outer circle, write possibilities that intrigue you but feel scary. This visual representation helps you see where fear might be limiting your choices.

Creating Your Purpose-Driven Plan

A plan without purpose is just a to-do list. Take time to create a meaningful path forward that aligns with your deepest values and aspirations.

Start by imagining your ideal impact— not just what you want to achieve, but how you want to affect others and the world around you.

Write about this vision in detail. What does it look like? How does it feel? What kind of person do you become in pursuit of this vision? Let yourself explore freely, without censoring or limiting your thoughts.

Navigating Setbacks with Purpose

Even when we're moving in alignment with our values, we'll still face setbacks and rejections. The difference is in how we handle them. When you're clear about your larger purpose, rejection becomes information rather than indictment. Each "no" helps refine your path rather than derail it.

Think of it like navigating by starlight. The stars remain constant even when clouds temporarily block our view.

Similarly, your purpose remains true even when rejection temporarily obscures your path. The key is maintaining connection with that deeper sense of direction while adjusting your course as needed.

Building Purpose Resilience

Develop what I call "Purpose Anchors"—statements that remind you of your deeper purpose: "I create value through..." "I make a difference by..." "My unique contribution is..."

These anchors help you stay focused on what matters most when rejection threatens to knock you off course.

Practice returning to these anchors daily, especially when facing challenges or setbacks. Let them remind you that your worth and purpose exist independently of any single outcome or person's response.

The Long-Term View

Adopting a long-term perspective helps you see rejection as part of your journey rather than its end.

Consider keeping a "Future Focus Journal" where you regularly write about your vision for the future. When rejection strikes, return to this journal to remind yourself of the larger story you're a part of.

Key Takeaways

1. Rejection can clarify what truly matters to us

2. Purpose provides direction beyond success or failure

3. Aligned action creates meaningful progress

4. Setbacks can strengthen our connection to purpose

5. Long-term vision sustains us through immediate challenges

Your Call to Action: The Seven-Day Purpose Path

Transform your relationship with purpose through daily practice:

Day 1: Value Clarity—Explore and document your core values and non-negotiables.

Day 2: Purpose Mapping—Create your three-circle Purpose Map, examining what drives you.

Day 3: Vision Creation—Write in detail about your ideal impact and contribution.

Days 4-7: Purposeful Action—Take one step each day aligned with your deeper purpose, regardless of potential rejection.

Remember: Moving forward with purpose isn't about avoiding rejection—

it's about being so connected to what matters that rejection loses its power to define you.

Each step aligned with your purpose strengthens your resilience and clarity, creating a foundation for meaningful action regardless of external responses.

Chapter 13: The Power of Positive Reframing

Rejection can feel like hitting a dead end, but it's often just a detour—a chance to discover a better path forward.

When we learn to reframe rejection, we transform what feels like a wall into a doorway. This isn't about denying the pain of rejection or pretending everything happens for a reason. It's about developing the ability to see opportunities within challenges.

Begin by considering your most recent rejection. Notice your immediate interpretation of this experience. Was it a final judgment on your worth? A sign to give up? A confirmation of your fears?

Write down your initial perspective. This becomes our starting point for learning the art of reframing.

Understanding True Reframing

Reframing isn't about forcing positivity or dismissing your feelings. Instead, it's about expanding your perspective to include possibilities you might have missed while focused on the rejection.

Think of it as turning on additional lights in a dark room—you're not denying the darkness exists, but you're choosing to see what else is there.

This process requires patience and practice. Start by examining one recent rejection from different angles.

What skills did you develop through this experience? What did you learn about yourself? What possibilities might this "no" open up that a "yes" would have closed off?

Moving Beyond Toxic Positivity

There's a crucial difference between authentic reframing and what's often called "toxic positivity."

Telling yourself or others to "just stay positive" or "everything happens for a reason" can actually prevent genuine processing and growth. Real reframing acknowledges the full experience—both the pain and the potential—while choosing to focus on what empowers us to move forward.

Consider a job rejection. Toxic positivity might say, "It wasn't meant to be!" and leave it at that.

Authentic reframing would acknowledge the disappointment while exploring what you learned from the experience, what skills you gained in the process, and how this might direct you toward an even better opportunity.

The Art of Perspective Shifting

Think of perspective like a camera lens. When zoomed in too close to rejection, all we see is the pain and disappointment.

But as we adjust our lens, pulling back for a wider view, we often discover aspects of the situation we couldn't see before.

Practice this lens adjustment daily. When faced with any kind of setback, consciously try viewing it from different distances and angles.

What becomes visible when you zoom out? What patterns or possibilities emerge from a broader perspective?

Creating New Narratives

Every rejection has multiple possible interpretations. Instead of accepting your first reactive narrative, practice creating alternative stories about what this experience might mean.

This isn't about finding the "right" story—it's about discovering more empowering ways to understand what happened.

Write three different versions of your rejection story:

1. From your current perspective

2. From the viewpoint of your wisest self

3. From the perspective of someone who deeply believes in your potential

Notice how each version feels different in your body. Which version energizes you? Which creates space for growth?

The Power of Questions

The questions we ask ourselves after rejection shape our experience of it. Instead of "Why did this happen to me?" try "What might this be making possible?" Instead of "What's wrong with me?" explore "What's this teaching me?"

Create what I call a "Question Compass"—a set of questions that guide you toward more empowering perspectives. Keep these questions handy for when rejection strikes.

Building Reframing Resilience

Like any skill, reframing becomes stronger through practice. Start with small rejections or disappointments.

Notice your automatic interpretation, then consciously practice finding alternative perspectives. This builds your capacity to reframe larger rejections when they occur.

The Integration Process

True reframing isn't just an intellectual exercise—it needs to be felt and integrated.

After exploring new perspectives, take time to embody the one that feels most authentic and empowering. Let this new viewpoint inform your next steps.

Key Takeaways

1. Authentic reframing honors both pain and possibility

2. Different perspectives reveal different opportunities

3. The questions we ask shape our experience

4. Regular practice builds reframing capacity

5. Integration turns insight into action

Your Call to Action: The Seven-Day Reframing Revolution

Transform your relationship with rejection through daily practice:

Day 1: Pattern Recognition—Notice and document your default interpretation of challenges.

Day 2: Perspective Expansion—Practice viewing one situation from multiple angles.

Day 3: Question Transformation—Create your personal Question Compass for future rejections.

Days 4-7: Active Reframing—Choose one experience each day to consciously reframe, noting how different perspectives feel in your body.

Remember: Reframing isn't about forced positivity—it's about expanding your vision to include both challenges and opportunities.

Each time you practice finding new perspectives on rejection, you strengthen your ability to use setbacks as stepping stones toward growth.

Chapter 14: Building Self-Esteem

Self-esteem isn't something that happens to us—it's something we build, choice by choice, day by day.

After rejection, this building process becomes especially crucial. While rejection can shake our confidence, it also presents an opportunity to develop a stronger, more resilient sense of self-worth.

Think of self-esteem like a house. Some people build their house on the shifting sands of external validation—success, approval, achievement.

When rejection comes, like a storm, it can wash away their foundation. But when we build our self-esteem on solid ground—our values, character, and inherent worth—rejection might rattle the windows, but the house remains standing.

Understanding True Self-Esteem

Many people confuse self-esteem with confidence or pride in achievements. But true self-esteem runs deeper.

It's about maintaining a stable sense of self-worth regardless of external circumstances. This kind of self-esteem doesn't crumble in the face of rejection because it's built on something more substantial than others' approval.

Begin examining your current foundation. What determines your sense of worth? Write down what makes you feel good about yourself.

Notice how many items depend on external validation versus internal values. This awareness becomes your starting point for building stronger self-esteem.

The Foundation of Worth

We often tie our worth to our performance, looks, or accomplishments. While these things matter, they shouldn't determine our fundamental value as human beings. Your worth isn't something you earn through success or lose through rejection—it's intrinsic to who you are.

This truth becomes especially important after rejection. When someone says no to your idea, project, or romantic interest, they're not rejecting your worth as a person. They're making a decision based on their own needs, preferences, and circumstances.

Understanding this distinction helps maintain healthy self-esteem even when facing rejection.

Building Internal Validation

One of the most powerful shifts we can make is moving from external to internal validation. This doesn't mean never caring what others think—we're social beings, after all.

It means developing the ability to validate ourselves rather than depending solely on others' approval.

Start by noticing how you talk to yourself. After rejection, do you become your own harshest critic? Or can you be a source of compassion and encouragement for yourself?

Learning to be your own ally rather than your own enemy is crucial for building lasting self-esteem.

The Practice of Self-Appreciation

We often find it easier to see worth in others than in ourselves. Yet building self-esteem requires developing the habit of acknowledging our own value.

This isn't about becoming arrogant—it's about being honest about your strengths, efforts, and growth.

Create a daily practice of self-appreciation. Each evening, write down three things you value about yourself that have nothing to do with external achievement. Focus on character traits, values, and qualities that rejection can't take away.

Growing Through Challenge

Rejection provides unique opportunities for strengthening self-esteem. Each time you face rejection and survive, you prove to yourself that your worth isn't dependent on others' responses. Each time you choose to try again, you demonstrate self-trust and courage.

Think of self-esteem like a muscle—it grows stronger when challenged, as long as we provide proper support and recovery.

Rejection can be that challenge, pushing us to develop stronger emotional muscles. The key is balancing challenge with self-compassion.

The Role of Self-Compassion

Self-compassion isn't self-pity or making excuses. It's about treating yourself with the same kindness you'd offer a good friend facing rejection.

When you stumble or face rejection, can you acknowledge the pain while still maintaining belief in yourself?

Practice speaking to yourself with encouraging honesty. Instead of harsh self-criticism after rejection, try saying, "This hurts, and that's normal. I'm proud of myself for trying, and I'll learn from this experience."

This balanced approach builds resilience while maintaining self-respect.

Creating Evidence of Worth

While your fundamental worth isn't based on achievements, building a record of personal growth and effort can strengthen self-esteem.

Start keeping an "Evidence Journal" documenting times you've shown courage, learned from mistakes, or persisted despite challenges. This evidence helps counter the negative self-talk that rejection often triggers.

Key Takeaways

1. True self-esteem comes from internal rather than external validation

2. Your worth exists independently of any rejection or success

3. Self-compassion strengthens resilience

4. Regular self-appreciation builds stable self-esteem

5. Evidence of growth supports self-worth during challenges

Your Call to Action: The Seven-Day Self-Esteem Strengthening Practice

Transform your relationship with self-worth through daily practice:

Day 1: Foundation Assessment—Examine and document your current sources of self-worth.

Day 2: Self-Talk Transformation—Notice and rewrite your internal dialogue patterns.

Day 3: Compassion Building—Practice responding to yourself as you would a dear friend.

Days 4-7: Worth Recognition—Each day, document three internal qualities you value about yourself, independent of external validation.

Remember: Your worth isn't determined by others' responses or any single outcome. Through conscious practice and self-compassion, you can build a foundation of self-esteem that rejection can't shake.

Each time you choose to value yourself despite external circumstances, you strengthen this foundation.

Chapter 15: Improving Social Interactions

After experiencing rejection, our social interactions often change in subtle but significant ways. We might become more guarded, hesitate to express ourselves fully, or read too much into others' reactions.

While these protective behaviors are natural, they can prevent us from forming the genuine connections we truly desire.

Take a moment to notice how rejection has influenced your social patterns. Have you been holding back in conversations? Analyzing every interaction for signs of potential rejection?

Write down how your social behavior has shifted. This awareness becomes our starting point for change.

The Hidden Impact of Rejection on Connection

Rejection leaves invisible fingerprints on how we relate to others. Perhaps you find yourself carefully measuring your words, waiting for others to make the first move, or maintaining emotional distance even in close relationships. These shifts might feel protective, but they often create the very distance we're trying to avoid.

Think about how water flows in a stream. When it hits an obstacle, it doesn't stop flowing—it finds new paths forward.

Similarly, rejection doesn't need to stop our ability to connect; it simply invites us to discover new ways of relating that feel both authentic and safe.

Rediscovering Authentic Communication

The art of genuine connection begins with understanding that everyone carries their own fears of rejection.

When you enter a conversation assuming others share similar human experiences, it becomes easier to relate authentically. This doesn't mean sharing everything with everyone—it means being real within appropriate boundaries.

Start noticing how different conversations feel when you're not trying to prevent rejection. There's a natural flow, an ease that comes from being present rather than protective.

This kind of authentic communication creates space for real connection, even if some people don't respond as we might hope.

The Power of Active Listening

One of the most powerful ways to improve social interactions is to develop your listening skills. When we're caught up in fear of rejection, we often listen through filters of anxiety or self-protection.

But true listening—being fully present with another person—creates opportunities for genuine connection.

Practice focusing completely on what others are saying rather than planning your response or worrying about how you're being perceived.

Notice how this shift in attention changes the quality of your interactions. Often, the more we truly listen to others, the more they open up to authentic connection with us.

Creating Safe Social Spaces

Just as you need to feel safe to open up, others need to feel safe to connect with you.

This doesn't mean never taking risks in relationships—it means creating an environment where genuine interaction can flourish.

Your consistent presence, reliability, and authenticity help build this safety in relationships.

When you demonstrate that you can handle others' authentic expression—including their fears, doubts, and imperfections—you invite similar acceptance of your own humanity. This mutual acceptance creates deeper, more meaningful connections.

The Art of Vulnerability

Appropriate vulnerability is like seasoning in cooking—the right amount enhances everything, while too much can overwhelm.

After rejection, we often swing between extremes: either completely closing off or desperately seeking validation through over-sharing. The key is finding balance.

Start with small moments of authentic sharing. Notice how others respond, not just in words but in their level of engagement and reciprocal sharing.

This gradual approach helps build trust—both in others and in your own judgment about when and how to be vulnerable.

Reading Social Cues Accurately

Rejection can make us hypersensitive to social signals, sometimes seeing potential rejection where none exists.

Learning to read social cues accurately—without the distortion of past rejections—becomes crucial for healthy interactions.

Pay attention to the full context of social situations rather than focusing solely on potential signs of rejection.

Notice both verbal and non-verbal communication, remembering that others' reactions often have more to do with their own circumstances than with you.

Key Takeaways

1. Post-rejection guardedness can prevent authentic connection

2. Active listening creates space for genuine interaction

3. Balanced vulnerability builds trust gradually

4. Accurate social reading requires moving past rejection filters

5. Creating safe spaces encourages mutual authenticity

Your Call to Action: The Seven-Day Social Connection Challenge

Transform your social interactions through daily practice:

Day 1: Presence Practice—Focus solely on listening in conversations, noting what you discover.

Day 2: Authentic Expression—Share one genuine thought or feeling with someone you trust.

Day 3: Safety Building—Create one moment where others feel safe to be themselves with you.

Days 4-7: Integration Practice—combining presence, authenticity, and safety-building in your daily interactions.

Remember: Authentic connection isn't about perfection—it's about being real.

Start where you are, with the people already in your life, and watch how small shifts in your approach transform your social experiences.

Chapter 16: The Power of Thinking and Mindset Shifts

Our mindset shapes not just how we see rejection, but how we experience it. The difference between seeing rejection as a dead end or a detour isn't in the rejection itself—it's in the lens through which we view it.

This chapter isn't about positive thinking; it's about developing a more empowering and realistic way of understanding rejection.

Think of your mindset like a pair of glasses through which you view the world. If those glasses are tinted with fear of rejection, everything you see will be colored by that fear.

But if your lenses are clear and balanced, you can see rejection for what it truly is—feedback, redirection, or sometimes even protection.

From Fixed to Flexible Thinking

A fixed mindset tells us our abilities and worth are set in stone—that rejection is a judgment of who we are.

A flexible mindset recognizes that we're constantly evolving, and rejection is simply part of that evolution. This shift transforms rejection from a final verdict into valuable feedback for growth.

Begin noticing when you slip into fixed thinking. Do you interpret rejection as permanent? Do you see it as a judgment of your character rather than feedback on a specific situation?

Write down these moments of fixed thinking—they become opportunities for developing greater flexibility.

The Stories We Tell Ourselves

Our minds naturally create stories to make sense of rejection. These stories can either empower or limit us. Notice what story you typically tell yourself after rejection. Is it a story of permanent limitation, or one of temporary setback and learning?

The key isn't to create artificial happy endings, but to recognize that we have choice in how we interpret and frame our experiences with rejection. The stories we tell become the reality we live.

Start paying attention to your default rejection narrative. Write it down, then practice creating alternative interpretations that feel both honest and empowering.

Embracing Uncertainty

Many of our fixed mindset patterns come from trying to create certainty in an uncertain world. We'd rather believe in a definite "no" than sit with the discomfort of "maybe" or "not yet."

But some of life's best opportunities emerge from embracing uncertainty.

Practice sitting with uncertainty in small ways. When faced with potential rejection, resist the urge to create immediate closure. Stay open to possibilities rather than rushing to conclusions. Notice how this openness creates space for unexpected opportunities.

Building Mental Stamina

Just as athletes build physical stamina through consistent training, we can build mental stamina through mindset practices.

Each time you choose a growth perspective over a fixed one, you strengthen your capacity for resilient thinking.

Create a daily mindset workout: Choose one challenging situation each day to consciously apply your growth mindset.

Notice how this deliberate practice builds your mental resilience over time.

Document your progress, celebrating small shifts in perspective.

Creating Supportive Thought Patterns

Lasting mindset shifts happen when we create new neural pathways through consistent practice. Think of it like establishing a new path through a field— the more you walk it, the clearer and easier to follow it becomes.

Start by identifying one limiting thought pattern around rejection. Each time it arises, consciously choose a more empowering alternative.

Write down both the old pattern and your chosen new perspective. Practice this shift daily until it becomes more natural.

The Power of Questions

The questions we ask ourselves after rejection profoundly influence our mindset. Instead of "Why me?" try "What can I learn from this?"

Instead of "What's wrong with me?" ask "What's next for me?" Create a list of empowering questions to turn to after rejection.

Practice using these questions daily, even with small setbacks. The more familiar you become with growth-oriented questioning, the more naturally you'll apply it when facing significant rejection.

Key Takeaways

1. Mindset determines how we experience and learn from rejection

2. Flexibility in thinking creates opportunity for growth

3. The stories we tell shape our reality

4. Embracing uncertainty opens new possibilities

5. Consistent practice creates lasting mindset changes

Understanding True Support

There's a common misconception that needing support means you're weak. Nothing could be further from the truth.

The most resilient people are often those who know how to build and maintain strong support networks. They understand that having people in your corner doesn't diminish your strength—it multiplies it.

Think of support like the roots of a tree. While a single tree might struggle against strong winds, trees that grow in groves support each other through their interconnected root systems.

Your support system works the same way, providing stability and strength during challenging times.

The Elements of a Strong Support System

An effective support system isn't just about having people around you—it's about having the right people in the right roles. Like a well-designed building, each element serves a specific purpose while contributing to the overall structure.

Some people will be your encouragers, always ready with a word of support. Others might be your truth-tellers, providing honest feedback when you need it. Still others might be your fellow travelers, sharing their own experiences with rejection and growth.

Start mapping your current support network. Who plays which roles in your life? Where might you need additional support? This understanding helps you strengthen your system intentionally.

Building Authentic Connections

Creating a support system isn't about collecting contacts or networking for advantage. It's about developing genuine relationships with people who understand and support your journey. These connections need to be nurtured with authenticity and reciprocity.

Begin with one relationship you'd like to deepen. Share something meaningful about your journey with rejection and growth. Notice how vulnerability, when offered appropriately, often strengthens connections rather than weakening them.

The Art of Asking for Support

Many of us struggle with asking for support, either because we don't want to burden others or because we're afraid of another rejection. Yet learning to ask for support directly and clearly is a crucial skill for building resilience.

Practice asking for what you need specifically. Instead of vague hints, try clear requests: "Could you listen while I process this rejection?" "Would you be willing to share how you handled a similar situation?"

Notice how direct requests often lead to more meaningful support.

Creating Support Rituals

Regular connection with your support system helps maintain its strength. Just as you might schedule regular maintenance for your car, schedule regular check-ins with key supporters. These consistent connections provide stability during challenging times.

Establish regular connection rituals that work for both you and your supporters. This might be a weekly coffee date, a monthly deep conversation, or regular check-in calls. The format matters less than the consistency.

Expanding Your Circle

While core supporters are crucial, don't overlook the value of wider connections. Support can come from unexpected places—mentors, peers, or even people who've faced similar rejections. Look for opportunities to expand your support network gradually and authentically.

Supporting Others

A strong support system works both ways. Being a supporter for others not only strengthens your connections but also develops your own resilience.

When you help others navigate rejection, you reinforce your own growth mindset and coping strategies.

Key Takeaways

1. Seeking support is a sign of wisdom, not weakness
2. Different supporters serve different crucial roles
3. Regular connection maintains support system strength
4. Clear requests lead to more effective support
5. Supporting others strengthens your own resilience

Your Call to Action: The Seven-Day Support System Building Challenge

Transform your approach to support through daily practice:

Day 1: Support Mapping—Document your current support network and identify gaps.

Day 2: Connection Initiation—Reach out to one potential supporter with authenticity.

Day 3: Clear Communication—Practice making one specific request for support.

Days 4-7: System Strengthening—Build regular connection rituals and deepen existing support relationships.

Remember: Creating a strong support system isn't about dependency—it's about creating a network of connections that help you become more resilient and capable.

Each step you take to strengthen these connections is an investment in your own growth and resilience.

Chapter 18: Recovery and Self-Healing Techniques

Just as an athlete needs recovery time after intense training, we need conscious healing time after rejection. This isn't about wallowing in pain—it's about giving ourselves the space and support needed to process, heal, and emerge stronger.

Recovery isn't a sign of weakness; it's an essential part of building resilience.

Think of emotional recovery like tending a garden. You can't force flowers to bloom faster by pulling on them, but you can create the conditions that support natural growth and healing.

The same principle applies to recovering from rejection. While we can't rush the process, we can create an environment that supports our natural resilience.

Begin by creating a dedicated recovery space in your home—a corner, room, or even just a comfortable chair where you can regularly check in with yourself.

Spend ten minutes there each day this week, simply being present with whatever you're feeling.

Understanding Your Recovery Rhythm

Everyone has their own natural recovery rhythm. Some people need immediate processing time after rejection, while others benefit from a brief distraction before diving deeper.

There's no universal timeline for healing, but there are universal principles that support it.

Start noticing your patterns this week. For the next three rejections you face, track how you naturally want to respond. Do you prefer solitude or connection? Movement or stillness?

Understanding these patterns helps you honor your unique healing process rather than forcing yourself into someone else's recovery mold.

The Body-Mind Connection

Rejection doesn't just impact our emotions—it affects our entire system. Our bodies often carry the tension of rejected experiences long after our minds have processed them. Learning to release this physical tension becomes crucial for complete recovery.

Next time you feel the sting of rejection, pause to notice where you hold tension in your body.

Is it in your shoulders? Your chest? Your stomach?

Practice gentle stretching or movement focused on these areas. Simple activities like walking, yoga, or even conscious breathing can help release stored tension.

The Healing Power of Nature

Nature provides powerful metaphors and medicine for recovery. The rhythms of the natural world remind us that periods of apparent loss or rejection often precede new growth.

The bare branches of winter eventually give way to spring's new leaves. The seemingly destructive forest fire creates conditions for new growth.

Make time each day to connect with nature, even in small ways. Sit under a tree, tend to a plant, or simply watch clouds move across the sky.

Let these natural cycles inform your understanding of rejection and recovery.

Somatic Healing Practices

Our bodies hold wisdom about what we need for recovery. Learning to listen to and honor these physical signals accelerates healing.

Start each morning with a gentle body scan. Spend five minutes moving your attention from your toes to the top of your head, noticing areas of tension or discomfort.

Let these physical signals guide your self-care choices for the day.

If your shoulders feel tight, perhaps you need movement. If your chest feels constricted, deep breathing might help. If your stomach feels unsettled, gentle nurturing might be the answer.

Trust your body's wisdom about what it needs for healing.

Creating Recovery Rituals

Just as we have morning routines to start our day, we need recovery rituals to process rejection.

These rituals provide structure and meaning to our healing process. They help us move from reactive pain to conscious recovery.

Design a simple five-minute recovery ritual you can practice daily. It might combine deep breathing, gentle movement, and positive self-talk.

The key is consistency rather than complexity. Practice your ritual even on good days—this builds the neural pathways that make it more effective when you really need it.

The Power of Creative Expression

Sometimes words aren't enough to process rejection. Creative expression—whether through art, music, movement, or writing—can access deeper levels of healing. You don't need to be an artist to benefit from creative recovery practices.

Choose one form of creative expression that feels natural to you. Spend fifteen minutes expressing your rejection experience through this medium. Don't judge the result—focus on the process of release and expression.

Building Your Recovery Toolkit

Think of recovery like having a first-aid kit for emotional wounds. Stock your toolkit with items and practices that support your healing.

This might include comforting music, essential oils, inspiring quotes, or photographs that remind you of your strength. Keep these easily accessible for when rejection strikes.

The Role of Rest and Renewal

In our busy world, we often try to push through rejection without taking proper recovery time. But just as sleep is essential for physical healing, emotional rest is crucial for rejection recovery. Create what I call a "recovery hour" for yourself each week. During this time, engage only in activities that restore and renew you.

Key Takeaways

1. Recovery is an active process requiring conscious attention

2. Each person has their own natural healing rhythm

3. The body holds wisdom about what we need for healing

4. Creative expression facilitates deeper recovery

5. Regular rest and renewal support lasting resilience

Your Call to Action: The Seven-Day Recovery Integration

Day 1: Recovery Space—Create Your Recovery Space Design and set up your dedicated healing space.

Day 2: Body Wisdom—Practice body scanning and responding to physical signals.

Day 3: Nature Connection—Spend time observing and learning from natural cycles.

Days 4-7: Full Integration—Combine all recovery practices, noting what works best for you.

Remember: Taking time for recovery isn't self-indulgent—it's essential for building lasting resilience.

Each time you honor your need for healing, you strengthen your capacity to bounce back from future rejections.

Trust your natural recovery rhythm and give yourself the time and space needed for true healing.

Chapter 19: Perseverance in the Face of Rejection

Perseverance isn't about never falling—it's about how you choose to rise again.

While talent, luck, and timing all play their roles in success, perseverance often makes the decisive difference between those who achieve their dreams and those who abandon them.

In this chapter, we'll explore how to cultivate the kind of perseverance that transforms rejection from a stopping point into a stepping stone.

The Nature of True Perseverance

Think of perseverance like water flowing downstream. When water encounters an obstacle, it doesn't stop or turn back—it finds another way forward. Sometimes it goes around, sometimes over, sometimes under, but it always continues its journey.

This is true perseverance: not the absence of obstacles, but the determination to find a way through or around them.

Your reflection moment: Think of a time when you persevered despite rejection. What gave you the strength to continue?

Write down three specific elements that helped you persist. This becomes your personal blueprint for perseverance.

The Persistence Paradox

Here's something fascinating about perseverance: the more you practice it, the easier it becomes.

Each time you choose to continue despite rejection, you're not just moving toward your goal—you're building your capacity for future persistence. It's like developing a muscle; each "rep" of choosing to continue makes you stronger.

Today's practice: Choose one small thing to persist with despite the possibility of rejection. It might be sharing an idea, making a request, or taking a creative risk. Notice how the mere act of continuing builds your perseverance muscle.

Strategic Stubbornness

Effective perseverance isn't about blind persistence—it's about strategic stubbornness. This means being flexible about your approach while remaining committed to your core goals. When rejection appears, ask yourself: "Do I need to change my method or just keep going?"

Your strategy check: Identify something you've been pursuing. Write down three different approaches you could take to reach the same goal. This gives you options when one path is blocked.

The Power of Incremental Progress

Major achievements rarely happen in one giant leap—they're usually the result of consistent small steps forward, even in the face of rejection.

Think of it like crossing a stream on stepping stones. Each small success creates a foundation for the next step.

Your daily stepping stone: Choose one small action you can take today toward your goal, regardless of past rejections. Document this step in your journey journal. Small wins build momentum.

Learning from Rejection Without Being Defined by It

Every rejection contains valuable information if we're willing to look for it. The key is extracting the lesson without internalizing the rejection as a judgment of your worth.

Think of rejection like a GPS recalculating your route—it's not telling you to abandon your destination, just to find a different way there.

After each rejection, ask yourself: What can I learn from this that will help me move forward? What adjustments might make success more likely next time?

The Role of Rest in Perseverance

Sustained perseverance requires strategic rest. Just as athletes need recovery time between training sessions, you need to pause and replenish your determination. This isn't giving up—it's gathering strength for the next push forward.

Create your rest ritual: Design a ten-minute daily practice that helps you recharge your persistence. This might be meditation, exercise, or simply quiet reflection on your progress.

Building Your Perseverance Network

No one perseveres entirely alone. Behind every story of individual persistence, there's usually a network of support. These are the people who believe in you when rejection makes it hard to believe in yourself.

Your support step: Identify three people who can support your persistence. Share your goals with them and let them know how they can help you stay determined when rejection hits.

The Long Game Mindset

Perseverance becomes easier when you view it as part of a longer journey rather than a series of isolated moments. Think of it like planting a garden—some seeds sprout quickly, others take time, but consistent tending eventually yields results.

Your long-term view: Write a letter to yourself dated one year from now, describing how your current persistence has paid off. Keep this letter where you can read it after future rejections.

The Courage to Begin Again

Sometimes perseverance means starting over with new wisdom. This isn't failure—it's evolution. Each time you begin again, you bring with you everything you've learned from past attempts.

Your fresh start practice: If you need to begin again, perform a small ritual that honors what you've learned and affirms your commitment to continue. This might be writing a reflection, creating a symbolic gesture, or simply stating your renewed intention.

Key Takeaways

Perseverance isn't about never feeling discouraged—it's about continuing despite discouragement.

Through conscious practice and strategic approach, you can develop the kind of persistence that turns rejection into a catalyst for success.

Your Call to Action: The 30-Day Persistence Project

For the next month, commit to building your perseverance through consistent practice:

Create a Persistence Journal where you track daily:

- One action you took despite fear of rejection

- What you learned from any rejections faced

- How you chose to continue moving forward

- Small wins and progress markers

Week 1: Focus on building your daily persistence habit

Week 2: Practice strategic adjustments to rejection

Week 3: Strengthen your support network

Week 4: Integrate lessons and plan long-term persistence

Remember: Every major achievement in human history came through persistence in the face of rejection. Your persistence isn't stubbornness—it's the key to transforming your dreams into reality.

Each time you choose to continue despite rejection, you're not just pursuing your goals—you're developing the kind of perseverance that defines history makers.

Chapter 20: The Power of Assertiveness

Fear of rejection often leads us to communicate in ways that undermine our needs and desires. We might become overly passive, aggressively defensive, or bounce between these extremes.

True assertiveness offers a different path—one where we can express ourselves clearly and confidently while respecting both ourselves and others.

Begin today by noticing how you typically communicate when you fear rejection.

Do you tend to shrink back, making yourself smaller? Do you push too hard, trying to prevent rejection through force? Or, do you withdraw entirely, avoiding the possibility of rejection by staying silent?

Write down your observations. This awareness becomes your starting point for developing authentic assertiveness.

Understanding True Assertiveness

Assertiveness isn't about being aggressive or demanding. Think of it like adjusting the volume on a speaker—too soft and you can't be heard, too loud and people cover their ears.

Assertiveness is finding that sweet spot where your voice is clear, strong, and effective.

Many people mistake assertiveness for confrontation, but real assertiveness actually reduces conflict.

When you communicate clearly and respectfully, you create space for genuine dialogue rather than misunderstanding or resentment.

Take a moment to recall a time when someone communicated assertively with you. How did it feel different from aggressive or passive communication?

The Foundation of Assertive Communication

At its core, assertiveness rests on a simple truth: your needs and feelings matter just as much as anyone else's—no more, no less.

This balanced perspective allows you to express yourself without either diminishing your own worth or overshadowing others.

Try this practice: Choose something you need or want. Complete this sentence: "I matter, you matter, and I need _____."

Notice how different this feels from either apologizing for your needs or demanding they be met. Practice saying this aloud, feeling the balance between self-respect and respect for others.

Finding Your Authentic Voice

Your assertive voice should sound like you—just a clearer, more confident version of yourself. It's not about mimicking someone else's style or forcing yourself into an uncomfortable mold.

Think of it as turning up the volume on your authentic self rather than trying to speak in someone else's voice.

Record yourself stating a simple need or boundary. Listen back. Does it sound like you? Does it convey both confidence and respect? Adjust until it feels authentically assertive.

Remember, your goal isn't to sound like someone else—it's to sound like the most clear and confident version of yourself.

The Art of Clear Requests

Many of us struggle with making clear requests because we fear rejection.

Instead, we hint, hope, or expect others to read our minds. Assertiveness means learning to ask for what you need directly while being prepared for any response.

Practice making clear requests by including these elements: what you need, why it matters, and the specific action you're requesting.

For example: "I need uninterrupted time in the morning to focus on my work. Could we schedule our team meetings for after 11am?" Notice how this differs from either hinting at your preference or demanding compliance.

Maintaining Boundaries Without Walls

Assertiveness plays a crucial role in boundary-setting. Think of boundaries like a garden fence—it clearly marks your space while still allowing for connection. Too many people either build walls (aggressive) or leave their space completely open (passive).

Start by identifying one area where you need stronger boundaries. Write out how you'll communicate this clearly and respectfully.

Practice saying it aloud until it feels natural. Remember that boundaries aren't about keeping people out— they're about defining the conditions under which genuine connection can flourish.

The Power of Peaceful Persistence

Sometimes assertiveness requires staying power—the ability to maintain your position calmly and consistently in the face of resistance. This isn't about wearing others down but about remaining steady in your truth.

When you face pushback against your assertive communication, practice restating your position calmly: "I understand you see it differently, and this is still important to me." Notice how this maintains your position while acknowledging the other person's perspective.

Navigating Different Contexts

Assertiveness looks different in various situations. What works in a professional setting might need adjustment in personal relationships.

The core principles remain the same, but the expression varies according to context and relationship.

Spend time adapting your assertive communication style for different situations. How might you express the same need differently to a boss, a friend, or a family member?

Practice these variations until you feel comfortable adjusting your style while maintaining your authenticity.

Key Takeaways

1. True assertiveness balances self-respect with respect for others

2. Clear communication reduces conflict and builds understanding

3. Authentic assertiveness sounds like you at your most clear and confident

4. Consistent practice develops lasting assertiveness skills

5. Context-appropriate assertiveness strengthens all relationships

Your Call to Action: The Seven-Day Assertiveness Integration

Day 1: Voice Discovery—Record yourself making simple requests, focusing on finding your authentic assertive voice.

Day 2: Clear Communication—Practice making one clear request, including what you need and why it matters.

Day 3: Boundary Expression—Choose one boundary to communicate clearly and respectfully.

Day 4: Peaceful Persistence—Practice maintaining your position calmly in the face of disagreement.

Days 5-7: Real-World Integration—Apply your assertiveness skills in increasingly challenging situations, starting with safe relationships and moving toward more difficult contexts.

Remember: Assertiveness is a practice, not a destination. Each time you express yourself clearly and confidently, you strengthen this skill, regardless of the outcome.

The goal isn't to never face rejection—it's to remain true to yourself while navigating life's inevitable nos and yeses.

Chapter 21: Integrating Rejection Lessons into Daily Life

Learning about rejection resilience is one thing; living it is another.

As we reach this final chapter, you might be wondering how to take all these concepts—from understanding your rejection response to setting boundaries, from processing emotions to building support systems—and weave them naturally into your daily life.

The key lies not in adding more to your already full plate, but in transforming how you approach each day.

Making Resilience Part of Your Natural Rhythm

Think of rejection resilience like breathing—it shouldn't require constant conscious effort. Just as you don't need to remind yourself to breathe, your resilience practices can become natural responses to life's challenges.

Begin by choosing one practice that resonates most strongly with you. Perhaps it's the morning body scan, the boundary check-in, or the gratitude practice. Make this your anchor habit, something you do automatically at a specific time each day.

Start small. Rather than trying to remember every technique we've covered, focus on integrating one practice fully before adding another. Notice how this single practice begins to influence other areas of your life naturally.

Creating Micro-Moments of Practice

Throughout your day, there are countless opportunities to strengthen your rejection resilience. While waiting for your morning coffee to brew, practice a quick body scan.

During your commute, notice and name any rejection-related thoughts that arise.

As you transition between tasks at work, take three conscious breaths.

These micro-moments don't require extra time—they fit into the spaces that already exist in your day. They remind you of your resilience tools while strengthening your ability to use them when needed.

Building Recognition Skills

As your awareness grows, you'll start noticing potential rejection situations before they arise. This isn't about becoming paranoid; it's about developing the capacity to prepare rather than react.

When you notice these moments, take a breath and remember: you have tools for handling whatever comes.

Practice recognition in low-stakes situations. Notice how you feel before asking for something small, like a coffee refill or directions. These minor moments become your training ground for bigger challenges.

Transforming Daily Interactions

Every interaction becomes an opportunity to practice rejection resilience. When expressing an opinion in a meeting, notice any fear of rejection that arises. When suggesting plans with friends, observe your reaction to their response. These everyday moments help you build strength for bigger challenges.

Start viewing each interaction through the lens of growth rather than protection. Instead of asking "How can I avoid rejection here?" ask "How can I stay true to myself regardless of the outcome?"

The Art of Recovery Integration

Recovery doesn't always mean taking a day off or having a long self-care session. Learn to integrate small recovery practices throughout your day.

Between meetings, take a moment to release tension from your shoulders. After a challenging interaction, step outside for a few breaths of fresh air.

Create what I call "recovery pockets"—
brief moments throughout your day
dedicated to releasing stress and renewing
energy. These might be as short as 30
seconds, but their cumulative effect is
powerful.

Celebration as Practice

Start celebrating your growth in small
ways. Notice when you handle rejection
differently than you would have before.

Acknowledge moments when you
maintain boundaries, express yourself
authentically, or recover more quickly
from setbacks.

Keep a "Growth Journal" by your bed.
Each night, write down one moment
where you demonstrated rejection
resilience. These recorded victories build
evidence of your growing strength.

Teaching Through Living

As you embody these practices more
fully, you'll naturally begin influencing

others. Without preaching or pushing, your example shows others a different way to handle rejection. When colleagues or friends notice your changed responses, share what you've learned if they're interested.

Remember that teaching often deepens our own learning. Each time you explain a concept or share a technique that's helped you, you strengthen your own understanding and commitment to the practice.

Creating Sustainable Change

The goal isn't to become immune to rejection—it's to develop a sustainable way of handling it that allows you to keep growing and pursuing what matters to you. This means being gentle with yourself when old patterns emerge while maintaining commitment to your new practices.

Think of your rejection resilience like tending a garden. Some days require active work, others just maintenance. The key is consistent, mindful attention rather than sporadic intense effort.

Key Takeaways

1. Integration happens through small, consistent actions

2. Every interaction offers a chance to practice resilience

3. Recovery can happen in brief moments throughout the day

4. Celebration reinforces growth and new patterns

5. Teaching others deepens our own practice

Your Call to Action: The Integration Journey

This week, begin your integration practice with intention:

Day 1: Choose Your Anchor—Select one rejection resilience practice to become your daily anchor.

Day 2: Map Your Moments—Identify natural opportunities in your day for micro-practices.

Day 3: Recovery Integration—Create three "recovery pockets" in your daily schedule.

Days 4-7: Living Integration—Practice weaving resilience naturally into your daily interactions.

Remember: True integration isn't about perfection—it's about progress. Each small moment of conscious choice builds your capacity for resilience.

As these practices become part of your natural rhythm, you'll find yourself handling rejection with increasing grace and wisdom, not because you're trying to, but because it's simply who you've become.

The journey of rejection resilience never really ends—it just becomes a more natural part of who you are and how you move through the world.

Keep growing, keep practicing, and keep celebrating your progress along the way.

Conclusion: From Rejection to Resilience— Your Continuing Journey

As we reach the end of this journey together, it's important to recognize that this isn't really an ending at all—it's a beginning. Throughout these chapters, you've developed a comprehensive toolkit for transforming your relationship with rejection.

You've learned how rejection affects your brain, your emotions, and your identity. More importantly, you've discovered how to turn these challenging experiences into catalysts for growth.

The Journey We've Shared (and all the lessons)

Let's take a moment to reflect on the key insights we've explored together. Here is a breakdown of the key lessons shared in each chapter of this book:

Understanding Rejection's Nature

We began by understanding that rejection isn't just an emotional experience—it's a biological one. Your brain processes rejection similarly to physical pain, explaining why it can feel so overwhelming. This knowledge helps normalize your responses and guides you toward more effective coping strategies.

The Science of Resilience

We explored how your brain can be retrained to handle rejection differently. Through consistent practice and conscious awareness, you can create new neural pathways that lead to greater resilience. Remember that each time you face rejection consciously, you're literally rewiring your brain for stronger future responses.

Processing with Purpose

You've learned that processing rejection isn't about rushing through the pain—it's about moving through it with purpose. The five stages of rejection processing provide a roadmap for turning painful experiences into valuable insights. This structured approach helps you avoid getting stuck while ensuring you extract meaningful growth from each experience.

Breaking Free from Conditioning

Social conditioning profoundly influences how we interpret and respond to rejection. By recognizing and questioning these inherited beliefs, you've begun freeing yourself from limiting patterns. Your new awareness allows you to choose responses that align with your authentic self rather than automated reactions.

The Power of Acceptance

True acceptance isn't about resignation—it's about acknowledging reality while maintaining your power to respond effectively. This fundamental shift in perspective transforms rejection from something that happens to you into something you can work with productively.

Building Resilience Through Practice

Resilience isn't innate—it's developed through consistent practice. The micro-challenges and gradual exposure exercises you've learned help build this crucial skill systematically. Each small win contributes to your growing capacity for handling bigger challenges.

Creating Authentic Connection

Rather than letting rejection drive you toward isolation, you've discovered how to use it as an opportunity for deeper connection. Authentic vulnerability and shared experiences create bonds that actually strengthen your rejection resilience.

Professional Identity Transformation

You've learned to separate your professional worth from individual rejection experiences. This crucial distinction allows you to maintain confidence while using feedback constructively for growth.

The Power of Boundaries

Strong boundaries don't limit connection—they make genuine connection possible. Your growing ability to set and maintain healthy boundaries supports both your resilience and your relationships.

Overcoming Limiting Beliefs

By identifying and challenging the lies rejection tells you, you've begun creating new, more empowering narratives. These truthful stories support your growth rather than limiting your potential.

Owning Your Story

You've discovered how to become the author of your own experience rather than feeling like a character in someone else's story. This shift in perspective gives you greater agency in how you interpret and integrate rejection experiences.

Moving Forward with Purpose

Rejection can actually clarify what truly matters to you, helping you align your choices with your authentic values and aspirations.

Building Self-Esteem

Your worth isn't determined by others' responses to you. Through consistent practice, you're developing a stable sense of self-worth that rejection can't easily shake.

Improving Social Interactions

You've learned how to maintain authentic connection even when facing rejection, creating stronger and more genuine relationships.

Mindset Transformation

Your growing ability to shift perspective allows you to see rejection as feedback rather than judgment, opening up new possibilities for growth.

Creating Support Systems

You understand now that seeking support isn't weakness—it's wisdom. Your intentionally cultivated support network strengthens your resilience while enriching your life.

The Power of Recovery

Through deliberate recovery practices, you're better equipped to bounce back from rejection while integrating its lessons.

Cultivating Perseverance

You've developed the ability to persist thoughtfully rather than stubbornly, knowing when to adjust your approach while maintaining commitment to your goals.

Assertive Communication

Your growing capacity for clear, confident communication supports both your resilience and your relationships.

Your Continuing Journey

The tools and insights you've gained aren't just for handling rejection—they're for building a more resilient, authentic life. As you move forward, consider how these skills apply to many areas of your life:

- Taking bigger risks in pursuing your dreams

- Building deeper, more authentic relationships

- Expressing yourself more confidently

- Pursuing meaningful goals despite obstacles

- Creating the life you truly want

Your Next Steps

1. Choose one principle from this book to focus on each month

2. Practice your new skills in progressively challenging situations

3. Document your growth and insights

4. Celebrate your progress, no matter how small

5. Share your learning with others when appropriate

Remember: Rejection will always be part of life, but it doesn't have to define your life. Through conscious practice and continued growth, you can transform rejection from something you fear into something that strengthens you.

The journey continues. Keep growing, keep learning, and keep transforming rejection into resilience.

Your greatest achievements may lie on the other side of rejection, waiting for you to be brave enough to continue despite the nos.

Trust in your journey. Trust in your growth.

And most importantly...

Trust in yourself.

As Always,

Scott Allan

About Scott Allan

Scott Allan is an international bestselling author of over 40 books published in 16 languages in the area of personal growth and self-development. He is the author of **Fail Big**, **Undefeated,** and **Do the Hard Things First**.

As a former corporate business trainer in Japan, and **Transformational Mindset Strategist**, Scott has invested over 10,000 hours of research and instructional coaching into the areas of self-mastery and leadership training.

With an unrelenting passion for teaching, building critical life skills, and inspiring people around the world to take charge of their lives, Scott Allan is committed to a path of **constant and never-ending self-improvement**.

Many of the success strategies and self-empowerment material that is reinventing lives around the world evolves from Scott Allan's 20 years of practice and teaching critical skills to corporate executives, individuals, and business owners.

You can connect with Scott at:

- www.scottallanpublishing.com
- www.scottallanbooks.com
- Join Scott Allan's Newsletter

Send an email to:

scottallan@scottallanpublishing.com

hello@scottallan.me

REJECTION FREE FOR LIFE

BY SCOTT ALLAN

www.ingramcontent.com/pod-product-compliance
Lightning Source LLC
Chambersburg PA
CBHW032054020426
42335CB00011B/334